The Shifting 21st-Century Presidency

The Shifting 21st-Century Presidency

ASSESSING THE IMPLICATIONS FOR
AMERICA AND THE WORLD

Edited by

Tevi Troy

University Press of Kansas

Published by the University Press of Kansas (Lawrence, Kansas 66045),
which was organized by the Kansas Board of Regents and is operated and
funded by Emporia State University, Fort Hays State University, Kansas State
University, Pittsburg State University, the University of Kansas, and Wichita
State University.

Library of Congress Cataloging-in-Publication Data

Names: Troy, Tevi, 1967– editor.
Title: The shifting twenty-first-century presidency : assessing the
implications for America and the world / edited by Tevi Troy.
Description: Lawrence, Kansas : University Press of Kansas, 2024. |
Includes index.
Identifiers: LCCN 2023031450 (print) | LCCN 2023031451 (ebook)
ISBN 9780700636464 (cloth)
ISBN 9780700636471 (paperback)
ISBN 9780700636488 (ebook)
Subjects: LCSH: Presidents—United States. | Political leadership—United
States—History—21st century. | United States—Politics and
government—21st century.
Classification: LCC JK516.S45 2024 (print) | LCC JK516 (ebook) | DDC
352.230973—dc23/eng/20231019
LC record available at https://lccn.loc.gov/2023031450.
LC ebook record available at https://lccn.loc.gov/2023031451.

Printed in the United States of America

The paper used in this publication is acid free and meets the minimum
requirements of the American National Standard for Permanence of Paper
for Printed Library Materials Z39.48-1992.

*To my children, Ezra and Ellie, Ruthie, Rina, and Noey,
whose generation will be inheriting this
new twenty-first-century presidency.
Good luck.*

Contents

A photo gallery follows page 65.

Acknowledgments

I express my deepest gratitude to the authors who submitted their papers for this project, including Kristen Soltis Anderson, Kenneth Baer, Jonathan Burks, Elaine Kamarck, and Martha Joynt Kumar. And I extend this gratitude to the nonpaper-writing participants, Josh Bolten, Jay Carney, Kellyanne Conway, Susan Glasser, Mack McClarty, Kelly O'Donnell, Jen Psaki, and Cedric Richmond, for generously offering their time and invaluable insight into the highest office in the United States. Without them, this exploration of the twenty-first-century presidency would not have been possible.

Thanks as well to the funders of the project, including the Achelis & Bodman Foundation, the Sarah Scaife Foundation, and An America United. Les Lenkowsky, a longtime mentor, was particularly helpful in coming up with the idea for this project, and Monty Brown has long been a source for inspiration.

The team at the Bipartisan Policy Center has been extremely helpful to this endeavor, starting with the indefatigable former president, Jason Grumet, as well as the new president, Margaret Spellings. Thanks go as well to Steve Scully, Kelly Darnell, Lisel Loy, Gwen Fortune-Blakely, Jason Fichtner, Dan Glickman, Tycely Williams, Luci Manning, Matthew Weil, Naleli Askew, Mike Vavala, Kurt Redenbo, Lauren Hopple, Agustina Pardal, Mary Margaret Holden, Alejandro Marquez, Audrey Cope, Elise Scott, Phenan Kidane, Kyle Huang, Jenn Ruff, and Greg Gibson.

I am grateful to the University Press of Kansas for publishing this book, and especially to David Congdon and Andrea Laws for all their good work. Thanks as well to Derek Helms, Erica Nicholson, and Suzanne Galle.

I would also like to give special thanks to my top-flight research interns, Chloe Kauffman, Kaelyn Milby, Ryan Nickol, Morgan Spencer, Krish Kothar, and especially Jake Walsh, for excellent work in helping me put this book together.

And finally, this project would not have been completed without the support of my wife, Kami, and our four—now five—children, to whom this book is dedicated.

The Rapidly Changing Twenty-First-Century Presidency

Tevi Troy

The presidency is an important and quintessential US institution. It can tie Americans together, lead America through times of crisis, and help to steer America away from authoritarianism on the right and socialism on the left. To do this, the presidency must maintain both its potency and its credibility. A weakened presidency can do very little, while a president without the respect of the American people is destined to fail. *For our nation to succeed, the presidency must maintain its characteristics as a respected American institution.*

Unfortunately, the presidency has taken some severe blows to its credibility in recent decades. Donald Trump was a norm-breaking president in a variety of ways, but he is far from alone in breaking established presidential practices in this century. Barack Obama had a "pen and a phone" presidency in which he promoted the use of executive orders and administrative action to accomplish what he could not get passed legislatively, even when he had previously said it was unconstitutional to do so. For his part, George W. Bush, with Congress, reorganized government to create the homeland security state in the wake of the September 11, 2001, terrorist attacks. He also alienated Democrats with his use of "signing statements" to explain his administration's interpretation of what legislation meant and how the administration would implement bills that had become law. And Joe Biden has sought to create New Deal– or Great Society–level changes of both a programmatic and a structural nature, with far narrower leg-

1

islative majorities than those enjoyed by ambitious presidents Franklin
Roosevelt and Lyndon Johnson. Furthermore, Biden declared a $500
billion student-loan forgiveness program, despite the fact that House
Speaker Nancy Pelosi, a fellow Democrat, specifically said that the executive branch lacked the power to do this.

The breaking of norms by each president in question is not necessarily alike. Some scholars have argued that Trump's actions were
the equivalent of amending the informal Constitution in at least five
significant ways. All presidents who have followed George Washington have either gone along with or away from the precedents that he
established. With the twenty-first century now more than 20 percent
completed, and in the context of a divided federal government and
populace, it is important to look at the changes to the presidency that
three consequential, but imperfect, presidencies have brought. As a
result of the changes wrought by three very different presidents, the
presidency inhabited by Joe Biden was significantly different in many
ways than the presidency Bill Clinton left at the beginning of 2001.

Although the presidency has always evolved, the rapidity of change
in just the first fifth of the twenty-first century is remarkable. Part of
these changes stem from the numerous crises of this young century:
9/11 and the resulting Global War on Terrorism, Hurricane Katrina,
the Great Recession, the coronavirus pandemic, and the urban unrest
of 2020. Crisis always brings with it rapid change. But there are other
factors at work as well. Increased polarization has led presidents of
both sides of the aisle to press existing rules and norms to their limits
in the short windows allotted to them. And advances in technology,
with the development of America as an impatient nation, means that
leaders feel the pressure to get more done during their tenures—
norms and rules be damned. The result is a lot of policy and structural
change in a short period, including new cabinet departments, new
election rules, and significantly increased spending and debt, among
other things. For the most part, these changes have occurred with
little thought to what it all means for the functionality and stability of
our democratic institutions and processes and, consequently, our nation's capacity to address the needs as well as aspirations of the American people.

These significant changes to the presidency are accretive. As the
presidency gains more power, it can use that power to implement
further expansions of the presidency and changes to our governing
structures. The changes also raise the question: Is the presidency as

currently configured reflective of its intended role as an American in-stitution? A number of scholars on the Right, including Chris DeMuth and Yuval Levin, both of whom have worked in the White House, have argued that Congress has ceded too much power to the executive. Con-gress passes broad laws but then leaves the details of the legislation to be worked out via regulation by the executive branch. Furthermore, Congress seems increasingly reluctant—or unable—to legislate, which leaves it to the executive branch to do more and more by executive action, an approach contrary to the one envisioned by the Founders.

At this point, twenty-plus years into the twenty-first century, it is an appropriate time to look back at the recent changes and see if they are what Congress and the American people want and if they correspond to the Framers' original vision of the presidency in our constitutional system. Many of these twenty-first-century changes have taken place in the wake of a crisis and in the midst of partisan warfare, so our nation has not taken stock of what the changes in toto mean for our polity and our nation. Examining these issues can help inform Congress, presidential aspirants, and the American people about the extent of the changes to our governing structures and begin to assess whether they have been helpful changes, and what can be done to reassert the proper balance of power among the branches of government if not.

These questions are particularly important in light of the interna-tional challenges we as a nation face. After a few decades in which democracy appeared to be on the march, it has receded in recent years, as more authoritarian systems in China and Russia have openly challenged American sovereignty. A system that relies too much on executive power and not enough on elected legislators has a weaker case to make in favor of the democratic way of life. Furthermore, the possibility of problematic leadership from the White House can affect America's global standing and its ability to make the case for democ-racy over authoritarianism.

Looking at important questions like these can help us determine if the presidency is situated better or worse as a result of these changes to lead our nation and the world through an increasingly uncertain future. With the input of major presidential scholars, experts, and administration aides from both sides of the aisle, this book begins to address these important issues. *The Shifting Twenty-First-Century Presi-dency* is based in part on the submitted papers and an edited version of the event proceedings of a series of conferences held at the Bipartisan Policy Center in the first half of 2022.

The goal of this gathering of presidential scholars and experts was to further the mission of the Bipartisan Policy Center's Presidential Leadership Initiative by forming a deeper understanding of perhaps the most powerful institution of the federal government. This volume examines the outsized and growing influence of the presidency and questions whether that trend is healthy to democracy in the United States and around the world. The point of the effort is to make observations that engage and include both citizens and policymakers in the political process regarding the state of the presidency. The participants all either have studied the executive branch extensively or seen how it operates up close while simultaneously having something original to say about it today. The aim of this project then is to allow them a platform to not only be contributors to this volume but contributors to the discourse that impacts the direction of our nation. The Bipartisan Policy Center is uniquely situated to engage in this effort, as it is respected by and holds credibility across the political spectrum.

Taking the ideas expressed in the chapters that make up this work and having them discussed by the authors should enhance the exposure of the recent developments regarding the modern presidency. As the presidency grows in scope, each president must juggle all of these increased responsibilities concurrently, potentially to the detriment of the ability to carry out the presidency's vast responsibilities in an effective manner. Regardless of party, the occupier of the White House and their administration must contend with battles being fought on many fronts. It is a necessity that the American public recognize this and be given the chance to reflect upon and determine if this is the government they want. With a populace that is continuously moving toward diverging poles, bringing luminaries from both sides together to discuss agreement on the job description and a rubric for grading of our presidents launches an important reexamination of the presidency. This nascent effort will make this title unique and the reading experience enriching.

The Management of the Presidency in the Twenty-First Century

My experience in the White House taught me that all White House work is funneled into two main buckets: president as decider and president as performer. The decider function is in essence about managing the vast apparatus that is the US federal government. Managing this behemoth requires a host of complicated decisions constantly being made by increasingly senior federal officials. The most complex and consequential of these decisions get made by the president of the United States. The processes by which these decisions get made are a key part of the management of the executive branch, and the subjects covered in this section—executive function, transitions, and foreign policy—are essential components of that executive branch management.

CHAPTER 1

Implementation Failure and Presidential Success

Elaine Kamarck

In 1789, Thomas Jefferson wrote a letter to the Frenchman Abbe Arnoux in which he concluded that "the execution of the laws is more important than the making of them."[1]

This has never been truer than it is now. In the twenty-first-century presidency—which exists in a maelstrom of commentary, some of which is serious, some of which is nonsense, and most of which is polarized—it seems that presidential performance is assessed on an hourly basis. And yet, as the saying goes, the more things change the more they stay the same. Even in an age of intense polarization, citizens' assessments of their presidents are fairly constant. Within what is a fairly narrow band, presidents suffer drops in their approval ratings. But some drops are larger than others and have longer-lasting and more serious consequences.

These policy shifts are complicated by the development that when presidents suffer implementation failures—in simple language, when stuff goes wrong—it takes a toll on the public's perception of presidential competence. As we will see, presidents lose political capital when the governments they run face implementation failures. This happened to George W. Bush after Hurricane Katrina, it happened to Barack Obama after the failure of the health-care websites, it happened to Donald Trump as he tried to navigate the COVID epidemic, and it has, once more, happened to Joe Biden in the wake of withdrawal from Afghanistan. In each instance, the political capital lost is nearly impossible to get back. For first-term presidents, implementation failures are major contributors to electoral failures. For second-term presidents, implementation failures eat up so much political capital that they are hobbled in their ability to enact the major changes they sought.

GEORGE W. BUSH AND KATRINA

Let's start with President George W. Bush's handling of Hurricane Katrina. On the afternoon of Friday, August 26, 2005, forecasters at the National Weather Service saw that a hurricane named Katrina was turning west. What they initially thought would be a Category 4 hurricane turned into a Category 5 and the mayor of New Orleans ordered the first ever mandatory evacuation of the city. Twenty-four hours later, things got even worse as the storm caused breaches in fifty-three different levees in the city, leaving 80 percent of the city underwater. Thus began a harried and ineffectual rescue effort that, in the days that followed, made the United States look like a third-world country.

For weeks, the rest of America and the world was treated to photographs of devastation. While much of the middle class had heeded the mayor's warnings and gotten out of the city, the poor were left behind, out of cash and with no money for bus tickets or for gas if they happened to own a car. (Since many poor people live from month to month on some form of government assistance, they had run out of money by the time the storm hit.) Some flocked to the Superdome, which, within hours, was overwhelmed with trash, backed-up toilets, and desperate people. Others found themselves on rooftops waving wildly at helicopters to be rescued from the rising waters. Emergency responders were themselves victims, and outside help was chaotic. The rescue efforts were characterized by "confusion, delay, misdirection, inactivity, poor coordination, and a lack of leadership at all levels of government," according to a subsequent congressional report on the tragedy.[2] As this was unfolding, President Bush traveled to New Orleans with the director of the Federal Emergency Management Agency (FEMA) Michael Brown and uttered the words that would come back to haunt him, "Brownie, you're doing a heck of a job." Twelve days later, Brownie was fired.

The damage to the Bush presidency was significant and impossible to fix. Katrina happened during the first year of Bush's second term in office. Given that his first-term goals had been upended by the attacks of 9/11 and the decision to go to war in Iraq, his second term offered an opportunity for him to make his mark on domestic policy. And, unlike 2000, in 2004 he had won a clean victory and control of both houses of Congress. He was thus poised to enact major policy. At the heart of his agenda was reform of social security through the establishment of personal savings accounts. As he began his second term, the White House outlined an ambitious campaign to convince the public and Congress of his plan. But after Hurricane Katrina, the political capital that he had intended to spend on this was gone. His approval ratings continued to deteriorate, the drive to reform social security fizzled, and Democrats won control of Congress in 2006 and the presidency in 2008.

OBAMA AND THE CRASHING WEBSITES

Bush's successor, Barack Obama, used up a great deal of his first-term political capital passing the Affordable Care Act. In the 2010 mid-terms, Democrats lost control of the House of Representatives and nearly lost control of the Senate. Nonetheless, Obama was able to win reelection and a shot at fulfilling the remainder of his domestic agenda, which included action on climate change he had abandoned in his first term. And then, in the fall of 2013, came the roll-out of his major legislative achievement, the Affordable Care Act (ACA).

On October 1, 2013, millions of Americans in search of subsidized health insurance logged on to the new federal website, HealthCare. gov, hoping to buy health insurance as easily as they could buy a plane ticket on Expedia or a book on Amazon. Or so they thought. Instead, to the dismay of millions of Americans shopping for subsidized health insurance—and to the surprise of President Obama and his top staff—the website crashed. Not once, not twice, but again and again and again over a period of two long months. The press erupted in a frenzy over the inability of the federal government, with all its vast resources, to build the website at the heart of President Obama's health-care re-forms. They were joined by a polarized citizenry, half of whom wanted to buy insurance and were endlessly frustrated and half of whom saw the whole episode as yet more evidence that the government couldn't organize a two-car funeral.

The impact on Obama's presidency was long-lasting. During the last three months of 2013, as stories about the troubled rollout of HealthCare.gov dominated the news, Obama's ratings fell to their lowest point ever, with only 39.8 percent approving of the job he was doing as president and 55.9 percent disapproving, according to an average of polls compiled by Real Clear Politics.[3]

Not only did the implementation failure fuel continued opposition to the ACA into the 2014 elections, it gave Republicans more ammunition against the Democrats, which they used in 2014 to win nine more seats in the Senate and thirteen seats in the House. This further doomed a slew of the president's other second-term initiatives, including immigration reform, climate change legislation, and gun control. The most Obama could do on many of these issues was to issue executive orders that were quickly rescinded when Trump took office. By the time Obama handed over power to Trump, his approval ratings had improved somewhat, but precious time had passed. Like his predecessor, Obama's implementation failure ended any change to enact significant changes in his second term.

TRUMP AND COVID

Donald Trump was a controversial president from the start—so controversial that his approval ratings never went above 50 percent in his entire four-year term in office. In fact, his average approval rating for his full term in office was the lowest since pollsters started measuring approval back when Harry Truman was president. But despite dismal approval ratings, an impeachment trial, and continuing controversy, as election year dawned, Trump's approval ratings ticked up and his reelection looked increasingly likely. Part of this was due to uncertainty as to who the Democratic candidate would be. Joe Biden, the most electable Democrat in a general election, was stuck in the polls and looking like he wouldn't even win the Democratic nomination. The momentum seemed to be with Senator Bernie Sanders—a socialist who many considered a sure loser in November despite temporarily polling well against Trump.

Republicans were predicting Trump would survive because of "progressive overreach" and a strong economy, not to mention the fact that the electoral college, with its heavy overrepresentation of rural states, gave Republicans a strong advantage. In addition to surviving an impeachment attempt, Trump had passed a large tax cut bill, he had an enormous war chest, and he had a united party. But most importantly, he had a booming economy, low unemployment, steady growth, and a healthy stock market. By January, the number of people reporting that they were satisfied with the way things were going reached its highest point since 2005.[4] Finally, he had the advantage of incumbency, and incumbents with strong economies rarely lose.

And then came COVID.

Trump's failures during the coronavirus pandemic ran the gamut from the rhetorical to the organizational. The White House Coronavirus Task Force was created on January 27, 2020, and chaired by Vice President Mike Pence. As the crisis deepened, Trump insisted on conducting a daily press conference on the situation himself. An anxious nation, stuck at home, tuned in faithfully, looking for solid information and for hope. Yet all too often when Trump went out to speak to the public about the crisis he added to the fear and chaos surrounding the situation. In the first month alone, he told Americans the pandemic was not serious by asserting his "hunches" about data,[5] he assured people that everyone would be tested even when there were very few tests available,[6] he told people that we were very close to a vaccine when it was nearly a year away,[7] he mistakenly asserted that goods as well as people from Europe would be forbidden from entering the United States,[8] and he announced that Google had a website for testing while the initiative was merely an unimplemented notion.[9] After each televised gaffe, a presidential "clarification" was needed. Trump had the unique distinction of giving a national address meant to calm the country that had the effect of taking the stock market down over one thousand points.[10]

But Trump's chaotic news conferences paled in comparison to the actual implementation missteps of his administration. The White House Task Force killed a plan to distribute masks to every household in America, a reflection of Trump's antipathy to masking. Trump refused to help governors who were in desperate need of ventilators, telling them that they should try getting it themselves.[11] By April, in the absence of a coherent plan for managing the national stockpile, governors facing shortages of equipment, from ventilators to personal protective equipment, were left to figure it out.[12]

One of the most glaring deficiencies was the failure to have enough tests available to identify those infected and to screen others for possible exposure. South Korea, a country a fraction of the size of the United States, was testing thousands more people a day than the United States.[13] The failure to produce tests quickly will go down as one of the biggest failures in the overall handling of this disease because it prevented authorities from understanding the scope of the pandemic and therefore made it difficult for them to undertake appropriate steps to mitigate its spread. Once again, governors were on their own, left to develop their own tests after the Centers for Disease Control and Prevention (CDC) belatedly removed regulatory barriers.

The one bright spot in Trump's implementation efforts was the plan to speed up progress on getting a vaccine. Named Operation Warp Speed, the massive effort coordinated by the federal government to produce a vaccine was modeled on the World War II war mobilization effort. It was wildly successful in developing and manufacturing a vaccine in less than a year. Trump tried in vain to hurry up the announcement of the vaccine, but it was not ready until after Election Day, and then it took months before supplies and distribution got straightened out. But by that time the election was over.

In what was shaping up to be a very close election, Trump's trouble managing the pandemic had a big impact on his reelection prospects. In April, Trump's approval rating was 47.4 percent, one of the highest in his presidency, but by July, as the pandemic went on and there was little or no tangible relief in sight, he suffered a 6.3 percent drop in the Real Clear Politics average of polls.[14] Of course, the most important poll took place on Election Day. Most of the voters who voted for Biden were casting votes "against his opponent."[15] Fully 60 percent of voters on Election Day said that the recent rise in coronavirus cases was the most important factor (23 percent) or an important factor (37 percent) in their presidential vote, and an overwhelming number of those voters voted for Biden. Nearly half of all voters said that "U.S. efforts to contain coronavirus are going very badly (32%) or somewhat badly (15%)." And on the question of who could "better handle the coronavirus pandemic," Biden ran ten percentage points ahead of Trump.[16]

BIDEN AND AFGHANISTAN

So now we turn to Biden. Biden began his presidency with a string of wins. He passed a massive COVID relief package through Congress.[17] Unlike Trump, who never fully embraced his powers, especially use of the Defense Production Act, Biden used that act and others to achieve large increases in vaccine production.[18] The federal government increased the supply of vaccines, and by spring of Biden's first year in office, state governments were, with the help of the feds, figuring out how to more efficiently get vaccines into arms. As William A. Galston

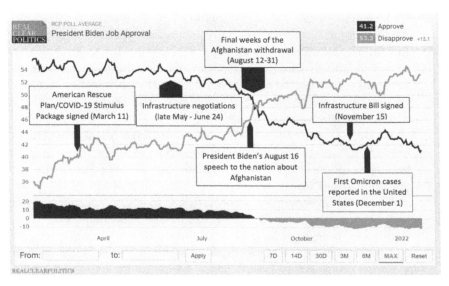

Figure 1. Biden Approval Polls.
Graph depicting the timeline of President Biden's job approval average for his first year in office. Courtesy of Real Clear Politics.

and I wrote in early May 2021, "In the past four months the COVID-19 vaccination campaign has gone from a desperate, chaotic search for scarce vaccines to enough vaccines for everyone who wants one."[19]

Thus, by the summer of his first year in office, Biden seemed to be doing fine. His approval ratings stayed above the 50 percent mark. He appeared to be fulfilling the expectations of the voters who had voted for him: he was able to pass legislation providing massive amounts of pandemic relief to the public (although he did not get any Republican votes for it). And he was getting vaccines into people's arms. The summer promised a return to normalcy.

But by August, the Biden administration was presiding over what looked to be a hasty and poorly planned exit from Afghanistan. For weeks in August, television footage of desperate Afghanis dominated the news. Many had cooperated in some way with the Americans during the long war with the Taliban, and we owed them protection against a Taliban with vindictive intentions. As they tried to get into the gate around the airport and board planes out of Afghanistan, Americans of a certain age were reminded of our equally chaotic withdrawal from Saigon at the end of the Vietnam War.

The Afghanistan withdrawal marked one of those massive implementation failures from which presidents have a hard time recovering. In Virginia, Terry McAuliffe was running for a second term as governor, and his campaign reported that during the summer they began to see "what they would later describe in a memo as 'a negative national climate'—collateral damage from the chaotic Afghanistan withdrawal, among other issues."[20]

Figure 1.1 illustrates what happened to Biden in his first year in office. Although his approval ratings had started to dip in the summer by August, his approval takes a dramatic dip downward as Americans are bombarded with news out of Afghanistan. Passage of the infrastructure bill in November is not sufficient to get his approval ratings back to where they were. By the beginning of his second year in office, Democrats were panicking over the upcoming midterm elections, and the Biden administration was promising a "reset." But nothing seemed to be working.

WHAT IS IT ABOUT IMPLEMENTATION FAILURES?

What is it about presiding over a major mess that is so damaging to the modern presidency? First and foremost, it erodes confidence in presidential competence. The fact is, Americans expect the president to actually run the executive branch of the government. When it fails, "the buck stops here," as President Harry Truman used to say. Presidents have a hard time predicting, understanding, and dealing with implementation failures because in the modern presidency, they are far removed from the operational side of the vast federal government that they are supposed to be running.

The Bush White House wasted several precious days before realizing that, during Hurricane Katrina, the first responders of New Orleans were also victims.[21] No one in the Obama White House was charged with writing the flawed computer code that took down the websites and frustrated millions of insurance seekers—but he got the blame. President Trump and his inner circle could not analyze emerging data on the COVID virus that caused so much confusion. And neither Biden nor anyone in his inner circle had experience in the huge military and logistical effort that Afghanistan turned out to be. Writing in his autobiography after he had left office, Bush had this to say: "Just as Katrina was more than a hurricane, its impact was more than physical destruction. It eroded citizens' trust in their government. It exacerbated divisions in our society and politics. And it cast a cloud over my second term."[22] This could be said of the implementation failures of all of the twenty-first-century presidents.

In every implementation failure, it's not too long before the initial shock and reaction is traced to large and expensive pieces of the US federal government that failed: the Federal Emergency Management Agency, the Centers for Medicare & Medicaid Services (CMS), the CDC, and the State Department and military. In each instance, there were warning signs that never reached the White House, resulting in as much surprise in the White House as in the public at large. The difference being, of course, that the public assumes the president is in charge and should have known.

CAN IMPLEMENTATION FAILURES BE PREVENTED?

The most common response of presidents to these large-scale failures is to concentrate on the unprecedented nature of the problem: a category five hurricane, a national insurance market run by the government, a worldwide pandemic, a large-scale evacuation. Everyone who finds themselves in this situation wants to argue that nothing better could have been done. And yet, the irony of a large and expensive government is that at any given point in time, something is going very wrong and something is going very right. In hindsight, it is almost always possible to find someone in the bureaucracy who saw the problem coming and someone in the bureaucracy who ignored the call to action.

This topic is too broad to go into in one essay. In fact, I wrote a book on this called *Why Presidents Fail and How They Can Succeed Again.* The book was published just as Trump got elected, but the Trump presidency and the Biden presidency have suffered the same fate as the two presidents I discussed. In all instances, the White House was so far removed from the federal agencies in charge that they failed to see the weaknesses that made the crisis response worse than it should have been.

Whether or not implementation failures are more prevalent in the twenty-first-century than they were in previous eras of US history is a tough question. The argument can be made that the failed rescue mission in Iran during Jimmy Carter's hostage crisis effectively sealed his loss in the 1980 election. But Ronald Reagan, George H. W. Bush, and Bill Clinton managed most of the next two decades without the types of implementation crises that have been discussed here. Another plausible explanation is that the first three presidents of the twenty-first century—Bush, Obama, and especially Trump—became president with far less governmental experience than their predecessors. Clinton was governor of Arkansas for over a decade, and Reagan's experience as a two-term governor of California, a state larger than most countries, is often forgotten in the mythology of a movie star president. But that can't explain Biden, whose extensive legislative and executive branch experience as vice president was a major reason why the country turned to him.

It is more likely that we are seeing these failures in the twenty-first century because for modern presidents, communications (fueled by things like social media and the twenty-four-hour news cycle) has taken precedence over governing. Understanding what the federal government can or cannot do and whether its parts have capacity if called upon to act are second- and perhaps third-order tasks for a modern president. They are programmed to be concerned with communication and message—not operations. What was Biden's reaction to the political situation he finds himself in at the one-year mark? He said he wanted to get out of Washington and talk to the country. Modern presidents and the closest people to them are experts in communication and either ignore or misunderstand organizational capacity. So far, no president has decided that instead of giving another speech he must figure out the weak links in the federal bureaucracy.

In all instances of implementation failure, the signals were there but they were ignored. The Federal Emergency Management Agency (FEMA) had been downgraded when it was placed inside the bureaucracy of the new Department of Homeland Security and its leadership was without emergency management experience. CMS was given responsibility for the ACA rollout even though it had been on the Government Accountability Office's (GAO) "high-risk list" of government agencies since 1990 and had had too many missions thrust upon it with too little organizational capacity. The CDC had severe data collection problems that emerged when the need for COVID data became acute in 2020 and the nation's public health infrastructure was well known to be seriously subpar.

Before the doomed August pullout of Afghanistan, the signals were there. According to John F. Troxwell, a professor at the US Army War College:

Compounding these general staffing issues, short tours of duty for both military and civilian personnel undermined institutional memory and programmatic continuity in Afghanistan. These tours, typically lasting less than a year for both civilian and military positions, limited the ability of staff to build a nuanced understanding of their role, their environment, and the Afghans they worked with. By the time they found their bearings and built important relationships, they began preparing to depart.[23]

Besides the general lack of expertise acquired for our efforts in Afghanistan, it may turn out that a major organizational failure was the failure to increase the capacity of something called OpMed in the State Department. The idea behind OpMed was to have a strong expeditionary force "dedicated to daring rescues of U.S. officials, American citizens, and foreign nationals imperiled overseas. . . . However, whenever OpMed offered options for evacuating AmCits [American citizens] and SIVs [special immigrant visas], 'They were told to sit in the corner and color,' said a source whose descriptions of meetings in June, July, and August was confirmed by three others."[24]

These are but a sample of the sorts of things to be found in hindsight. It will take a book or two to dig deep into what happened in Trump's pandemic and what happened in Biden's Afghanistan departure. Often this is done by a high-level commission formed by Congress. The lesson from the past is that in every instance, there are bureaucratic dysfunctions that were knowable but that never rose to the level of the presidency.

CONCLUSION

As all modern American presidents have learned, the world is a dangerous and totally unpredictable place. And yet, the problem is not that the modern federal government does too much. In fact, it is enormous and can do some pretty amazing things such as refueling aircraft while flying over the Atlantic, taking out terrorists from drones flying thousands of feet overhead, or developing a vaccine for a new virus in under a year.

In the face of these disasters, wouldn't it be great if, the next time an US president faces a crisis where some piece of the government fails, instead of going to the country to give a speech, they take some time to ask: What went wrong? What did we know? And how can we fix it? And wouldn't it be even better if, instead of (or in addition to) building a White House staff dedicated to polling and speech-making, the president took an interest in finding out the weak spots in their government that need fixing before they need to intervene in a crisis? Until this becomes an important part of the White House operation, presidents will falter at the hands of implementation failures that all the speeches in the world cannot correct.

NOTES

1. "From Thomas Jefferson to the Abbé Arnoux, 19 July 1789," Founders Online, accessed August 16, 2022, http://founders.archives.gov/documents/Jefferson/01–15–02–0275.

2. *A Failure of Initiative: The Final Report of the Select Bipartisan Committee to Investigate the Preparation for and Response to Hurricane Katrina,* House Report, 109th Cong., 2nd Sess. (Washington, DC: Government Printing Office, 2006), 109–377.

3. "President Obama Job Approval," Real Clear Politics, accessed July 13, 2023, https://www.realclearpolitics.com/epolls/other/president_obama_job_approval-1044.html.

4. Jefferey Jones, "Trump Job Approval Steady at 49%," Gallup, February 20, 2020, https://news.gallup.com/poll/286280/trump-job-approval-steady.aspx.

5. Quint Forgey, "Trump Floats His Own Coronavirus Hunches on 'Hannity,'" *Politico,* March 5, 2020, https://www.politico.com/news/2020/03/05/trump-disputes-coronavirus-death-rate-121892.

6. Noah Weiland, "Anyone Who Wants a Coronavirus Test Can Have One, Trump Says. Not Quite, Says His Administration," *New York Times,* March 7, 2020, https://www.nytimes.com/2020/03/07/us/politics/trump-coronavirus-messaging.html.

7. Elyse Samuels, "Trump's Inaccurate Coronavirus Vaccine Timeline," *Washington Post,* March 4, 2020, https://www.washingtonpost.com/politics/2020/03/04/fact-checking-trumps-accelerated-timeline-coronavirus-vaccine/.

8. Politi, James, "Trump Forced to Clarify Europe Travel Restriction over Cargo Claim," Financial Times, March 12, 2020, https://www.ft.com/content/e5efafc0–6419–11ea-b3f3-fe4680ea68b5.

9. Todd Spangler, "Google Not Launching a Coronavirus Testing Site as Trump Claimed—Variety," *Variety,* March 13, 2020, https://variety.com/2020/digital/news/google-site-coronavirus-testing-trump-1203533916/.

10. Fred Imbert, "Dow Futures Drop 1,100 Points as Trump Speech Fails to Calm Investors Rattled by Coronavirus Fears," NBC News, March 12,

2020, https://www.nbcnews.com/business/markets/dow-futures-drop-1–100 -points-trump-speech-fails-calm-n1156291.

11. Jonathan Martin, "Trump to Governors on Ventilators: 'Try Getting It Yourselves,'" *New York Times*, March 16, 2020, https://www.nytimes.com /2020/03/16/us/politics/trump-coronavirus-respirators.html.

12. "Governors Forced to Get Creative to Procure Ventilators in Face of Haphazard Federal Distribution," Kaiser Health News, April 13, 2020, https://khn.org/morning-breakout/governors-forced-to-get-creative-to-pro cure-ventilators-in-face-of-haphazard-federal-distribution/.

13. Anthony Kuhn, "Testing for Coronavirus in South Korea: Just Pull up at a Drive-through Center: Goats and Soda," NPR, March 13, 2020, https:// www.npr.org/sections/goatsandsoda/2020/03/13/815441078/south-koreas -drive-through-testing-for-coronavirus-is-fast-and-free.

14. "President Trump Job Approval," Real Clear Politics, accessed July 13, 2023, https://www.realclearpolitics.com/epolls/other/president_trump_job _approval-6179.html.

15. "2020 Exit Polls," CNN Politics, accessed July 13, 2023, https://www .cnn.com/election/2020/exit-polls/president/national-results.

16. "2020 Exit Polls."

17. The American Rescue Plan passed on March 11, 2021.

18. For a detailed explanation of the steps taken to increase vaccine produc- tion see Shayan Karbassi, "Understanding Biden's Invocation of the Defense Production Act," *Lawfare* (blog), August 31, 2021, https://www.lawfareblog .com/understanding-bidens-invocation-defense-production-act.

19. William A. Galston and Elaine Kamarck, "COVID-19 Vaccines: The Endgame," *Brookings* (blog), May 12, 2021, https://www.brookings.edu/blog /fixgov/2021/05/12/covid-19-vaccines-the-endgame/.

20. Ashley Parker, Tyler Pager, and Sean Sullivan, "The Long Slide: Inside Biden's Declining Popularity as He Struggled with Multiple Crises," *Washington Post*, January 19, 2022, https://www.washingtonpost.com/politics/biden-de cline-first-year/2022/01/18/19ecd8c0–7557–11ec-8ec6–9d61f7afbe17_story .html.

21. Elaine Kamarck, "When First Responders Are Victims: Rethinking Emergency Response," *Harvard Law & Policy Review Online* 1, no. 1 (2007).

22. Susan Walsh, "George W. Bush Never Recovered Politically from Kat- rina," Nola, August 28, 2015, https://www.nola.com/news/article_9b0ff883 –2078–5662–8e6b-b8296249a161.html.

23. "A Glass Half Full," Strategic Studies Institute, July 2010, 73; former senior DOD official, Special Inspector General for Afghanistan Reconstruc- tion (SIGAR) interview, September 14, 2015.

24. Adamn Ciralsky, "How Turf Wars Mucked up America's Exit from Afghanistan," *Vanity Fair*, August 30, 2021, https://www.vanityfair.com/news /2021/08/how-turf-wars-mucked-up-americas-exit-from-afghanistan.

CHAPTER 2

Presidential Transitions in the Twenty-First Century

Martha Joynt Kumar

In 2021, the efficacy of the Presidential Transition Act of 1963, along with practices associated with the presidential transfer of power, faced their most challenging test with an insurrection meant to halt the presidential transition process. On January 6, as members of Congress gathered in the Senate chamber, listening as Vice President Mike Pence presided, members of the House and Senate read out reports of state-certified electoral vote counts. In midafternoon, the quiet was shattered by the sounds, and later the presence, of a rioting mob trying to stop the certification process. Senate Minority Leader Mitch McConnell later described the scene: "We saw it happen. It was a violent insurrection for the purpose of trying to prevent the peaceful transfer of power after a legitimately certified election, from one administration to the next. That's what it was."[1]

Yet, in the midst of a volatile situation, where the incumbent president refused to concede and, further, called on his supporters to come to Washington to protest the certification of Joseph Biden as president of the United States, two weeks later, Biden was inaugurated the forty-sixth president. The scene on Capitol Hill that day was a peaceful one. In the twenty-four hours following his inauguration, President Biden swore-in his White House staff of over two hundred members, issued over thirty executive orders, and took actions related to climate change as well as reversing a host of Trump-era executive actions, such as Trump's order withdrawing from the Paris Climate Agreement and from membership in the World Health Organization.

The question presented here is how was Joseph Biden able to take office in what was a calm scene and with executive branch officials ready to carry out his calls for executive actions and members of the Senate ready to consider his nominees for Cabinet positions?[2] The public graded his transition into office with a 57 percent job approval rating.[3] The answer lies in a gradual recognition during the preceding sixty years that presidential transition preparations were properly the responsibility of government, not the political parties then funding the transfer of power. During the period from 1962, when presidential transition legislation was first considered by both houses of Congress, and Biden's taking the presidential oath, the actions of all divisions of government led to presidential transitions becoming a first order of federal government business.

The twenty-first century has seen development in the process through which presidents transfer power. When compared with the provisions of the first laws declaring presidential transition expenses as a government responsibility, the basic 1963 Presidential Transition Act has been updated to provide

- preelection funding of the two major party candidates following the national party nominating conventions,
- increased services with an emphasis on cybersecurity,
- early security clearances for select transition staff, and
- an executive branch organizational structure—a White House Transition Coordinating Council and an Agency Transition Directors Council—to handle transition planning and implementation.

As transition law has expanded its reach, transition sponsors included restrictions on where private money originates and established reporting requirements. Transition law developed through the support of a bipartisan coalition of lawmakers as well as presidents and executive branch officials involved in the process.

Transition law has been a last bastion of bipartisanship in a politically charged US political system. It remains so and, with a bipartisan commitment to the success of presidential transitions, the transfer of power from one administration to another has met with the challenges found in that passage from one president to another and, often, one party to another. That commitment to bipartisan transition arrangements remains, even if the public discourse surrounding the transition in 2020 was acrimonious.

In the twenty-first century United States, five people have served at least some time as president. They are Bill Clinton, whose term ended at the beginning of the century, George W. Bush, Barack Obama, Donald Trump, and Joseph Biden. The transitions involved here are 2001, 2009, 2017, and 2021. Of those four transitions, only the one in 2009 took place without controversy and even it faced a deadly threat on the inauguration presented by a nonstate terrorist group. A "smooth transition" was a goal for President Harry Truman, who first considered such a transition a necessity in our modern governmental system with the security threats the country faced, but in the twenty-first century, it is more an ideal than a reality. The mitigating factors working against a chaotic passage of power are transition law; the tacit understandings outgoing and incoming presidents have subscribed to; and the discretion the law allows for presidents, their White House staff members, and administration officials to go beyond the law to respond to current national security and domestic needs. All three—transition law, tacit understandings, and discretion—have combined to create a strong transition framework capable of responding to the threats that the political system has confronted in the twenty-first century. The people implementing transition, especially career staff in the departments and agencies, rely on all three elements as they handle transition planning.

PRESIDENTIAL TRANSITIONS IN THE TWENTY-FIRST CENTURY: TRANSITION LAW AND ITS ESTABLISHED PRECEDENTS

Bipartisanship has been one of the keys to the success of transition legislation. From its beginnings in 1962 from a bill dealing with political funding reform, members of Congress in both houses and in both parties have supported funding for presidential transitions primarily in a bipartisan manner. During the sixty years of transition discussion, Congress and the president have expanded the reach of transition called for with

- increases in funding and additional resources, particularly those related to cybersecurity;
- mandated financial disclosures by the candidates and then the president-elect and their team;

- limitations on the amounts private funders can provide to a candidate transition organization; and
- additional government institutions with transition responsibilities, such as the Office of Government Ethics.

The General Services Administration (GSA) was assigned the primary responsibility for transition preparations. While GSA remains at the core of a transition, today a presidential transition is an all-of-government operation.

While Congress was the lead institution shaping transition responsibilities, now presidents play a key role in leading departmental preparations. More active and earlier transition preparations result from several factors:

- An increase in presidential interest in shaping a transition
- Developments in the political environment calling for preelection transition planning, especially in the areas of national security, computer security, and the vetting of potential nominees for government positions
- Post-9/11 national security concerns calling for participation of additional government agencies and units in transition planning, such as the Office of the Director of National Intelligence and the Homeland Security adviser in the National Security Council
- Developments rising out of transition experiences requiring alterations in the law, such as placing limitations on transition funding by individuals
- An increase in the complexity of government, with national security being the top concern

The two branches have constructed a transition framework that places onus on the major party-nominating conventions and provides funds to both party candidates, not just a president-elect.

PRESIDENT TRUMAN: THE BRIDGE BETWEEN INFORMAL AND FORMAL PRESIDENTIAL TRANSITIONS

Prior to Truman's administration, presidential transitions were an ad hoc operation based on what the incumbent president believed to be his responsibility preparing a successor for the office. Presidents-elect along with their political parties decided what level of resources they wanted to provide for the incoming president. Through personal experience, Truman designed a transition where both major party candidates would come into office aware of security concerns. When Truman came into office on April 12, 1945, following President Franklin D. Roosevelt's death, he was unaware of the most consequential military program then underway: the Manhattan Project to build an atomic bomb. Truman was scarred by his lack of knowledge and wanted to make certain he did not leave his successor in the same position. Kenneth Hechler, a Truman senior White House aide, recalled the meeting Truman had March 29, 1952, the day following his announcement that he would not run for reelection:

> Now, whoever's elected this fall, whether he be a Republican
> or a Democrat, I don't want him to face the kind of thing that I
> faced when I came into office in 1945, completely unbriefed and
> unprepared, . . . I want this to be a smooth transition, whether it
> be a Republican or Democrat that's going to take over after next
> January 20th. I want everybody to work very hard on it between
> now and next January.[4]

For his part following the major party-nominating conventions, Truman wanted to brief the Republican and Democratic candidates, Dwight D. Eisenhower and Adlai Stevenson, in order for them to be current on national security issues. In mid-August, Truman invited the two candidates to come to the White House for a series of briefings, meetings, and lunch. His message to Eisenhower read:

> I would be most happy if you would attend a Cabinet luncheon
> next Tuesday the nineteenth. If you want to bring your press
> secretary and any other member of your staff I'll be glad to have
> them. If you can arrive at about twelve fifteen I'll have General
> Smith and the Central Intelligence Agency give you a complete
> briefing on the foreign situation. Then we will have luncheon
> with the Cabinet and after that if you like I'll have my entire staff
> report to you on the situation in the White House and in that
> way you will be entirely briefed on what takes place. I've made
> arrangements with the Central Intelligence Agency to furnish you
> once a week with the world situation as I also have for Governor
> Stevenson.[5]

Eisenhower turned down the invitation, but Truman had already set a precedent of going beyond law for a president to use his discretion to do what he thought was called for to prepare a candidate for the presidency. What Truman did was acknowledge the important difference between campaigning and governing with the need to get off to a quick and strong start. The eighty-three days he had to acclimate to the presidency did not prove to be sufficient to adequately prepare to handle the presidential responsibilities that came to him on April 12, 1945. The precedent he established of early preparation of presidential candidates led to transition discussions in 1962 and then basic transition law with the 1963 Presidential Transition Act. Additionally, and equally important, his transition-preparation efforts throughout 1952 underscored the importance of presidential discretion in adjusting preparations for a transition out of office, with an acknowledged respect for the office of the presidency and the well-being of the political system. In his response to Eisenhower's letter rejecting the luncheon invitation, Truman regarded Eisenhower as having rejected the notion of a bipartisan foreign policy, a necessity in Truman's view. "Partisan politics should stop at the boundaries of the United States," Truman wrote: "I am extremely sorry that you have allowed a bunch of screwballs to come between us. You have made a bad mistake and I'm hoping it won't injure this great Republic."[6]

FORMAL TRANSITION LEGISLATION: THE PRESIDENTIAL TRANSITION ACT OF 1963

The discussion of transition legislation began in 1962 with a reform proposal for campaign spending. The link between campaign spending and transition was the funding of transitions by political parties. Representative Dante Fascell [D-FL], the sponsor of reform legislation, spoke of the need for transition legislation. While Presidents Truman and Eisenhower provided information for incoming Presidents Eisenhower and Kennedy, Fascell spoke of problems that might in the future interfere with a cooperative transition between incoming and outgoing chief executives. He remarks that Eisenhower and Kennedy had

> the cooperation of their predecessors and access to what information they needed. This is as it should be. But the time has come to formalize the process. That is the purpose of this bill. To

leave these matters to the discretion of the existing President and the President-elect could conceivably have unfortunate results— especially if the incumbent was defeated by the President-elect in a hard-fought campaign. Let us guard against the possibility of noncooperation, remote as it may be.[7]

The legislation that prevailed provided

- $900,000 for the incoming and outgoing presidents without specifying how the funds were to be divided between them;
- federal government support for office space, staff, transportation, and services;
- determination from the GSA administrator of the "apparent successful candidates for the office"; and
- a president-elect's choice of whether to take transition support, as funding is voluntary.

Additional provisions were added to the original 1963 Presidential Transition Act. In 1978, the US Office of Government Ethics was added as a partner in the transition process, working through the financial disclosure process with nominees. When presidents-elect believed they needed additional funding beyond what the government provided, they turned to private funding. At that point, Congress patched the 1963 law with the Presidential Transitions Effectiveness Act of 1988. Congress required reporting of private funds, including in-kind contributions.

PRESIDENTIAL TRANSITIONS IN THE TWENTY-FIRST CENTURY: FACING LEGAL AND POLITICAL CHALLENGES

In the period from Truman forward, there were no serious challenges involved in deciding who won the presidential election. Eisenhower, John F. Kennedy, Lyndon B. Johnson, Richard Nixon, Jimmy Carter, Ronald Reagan, and George H. W. Bush all won without contest and with the losing candidate quickly conceding without incident. For the twenty-first century presidents, only Barack Obama won the election without a legal contest and with the support from the incumbent president, George W. Bush. In 2000, George W. Bush was not declared by the administrator of GSA, David Barrum, to be the winning candidate until the Supreme Court ruled in *Bush v. Gore* that the hand recount of "undervotes" ballots then underway did not need to proceed. From November 4 until December 13, there was no declared winner, as Florida, with less than one thousand votes separating Bush and Al Gore, had no settled winner. Under Florida law, less than one thousand votes called for a recount. The Associated Press, a traditional voice listened to by the administrator, did not call the 2000 election until after the Supreme Court rendered its decision on December 12. Vice President Gore conceded the following day, and then David Barrum, as the administrator of GSA, declared George Bush as the president-elect on December 13. That left president-elect Bush thirty-seven days to prepare for the presidency.

On November 27, after the election but before the Supreme Court decision, President Clinton stepped into the postelection phase with actions of his own. He issued an executive order creating a Presidential Transition Coordinating Council that brought together government departments and agencies central to a transition. The order provided for specific kinds of information to be provided by GSA, the Office of Personnel Management, and the National Archives. Most important, the council was tasked with supporting the president-elect and his team. According to the order:

> The Council shall coordinate assistance to the President-elect in fulfilling his responsibilities and make every reasonable effort to facilitate the transition between administrations. This assistance may include, among other things, providing publicly available information relevant to facilitating the personnel aspects of a presidential transition and such other information that, in the Council's judgement, is useful and appropriate as long as providing such information is not otherwise prohibited by law.[8]

The Council Clinton established by executive order was repeated by President Bush as he left office and then by President Obama. Regarded as a successful addition to the presidential transition process, Congress included the Council in its 2015 Edward "Ted" Kaufman and Mike Leavitt Presidential Transitions Improvements Act. The council and further developments requiring presidential initiative brought the president into the process as a central actor.

THE AFTERMATH OF THE 2000 ELECTION AND
THE 2001 TERRORIST ATTACKS

While President Clinton had White House and administration officials gathering information for whomever was declared the winner, George W. Bush had no access to the government services and office space provided for in the Presidential Transition Act. Bush raised funds to rent office space in McLean, Virginia, in order for his transition appointees to begin their work. Based on the election experience Bush faced and the 9/11 attacks months right after he came into office, there was a growing understanding of the fragile nature of the period of time between the election and the inauguration of a new president, as well as the early months in office.

At the time of the September 11 attacks, there were vacancies in administration leadership positions in the national security area. The 9/11 Commission took note of the lack of confirmed officials at the department and agency leadership level and called for early national security clearances for those working for the president-elect. The 2004 Intelligence Reform and Terrorism Prevention Act arranged for the presidential candidates to submit the names of people they wanted to have work on their transition should they win the presidency. With their clearances ready, agency team members responsible for review could begin their work gathering budget, program, and personnel information in the departments and agencies. The Obama transition operation submitted names of over two hundred people who they wanted to have security clearances in order to begin their work as soon as the election was called in Obama's favor.

With the understanding that a president-elect needs more lead time to prepare for office than the approximately seventy-five-day period between the election and the inauguration, Congress moved up the transition time clock. The 2010 Pre-Election Presidential Transition Act calls on the General Services Administration to provide the major party presidential nominees with office space, secure technology, resources, and information on government positions. Six months before, and then again three months before, the election, the federal transition coordinator on behalf of the president reports to Congress on the steps taken by the presidential candidates. They also receive national security briefings. Additionally, the act provides that a president "may" create a Transition Coordinating Council and an Agency Transition Directors Council. When he ran for reelection in 2012, however, President Obama chose not to create such councils. The latest major elements filling in the transition framework come out of the Edward "Ted" Kaufman and Mike Leavitt Presidential Transitions Improvements Act. It provides that the president "must" create a White House Transition Coordinating Council to develop transition policy and create a permanent Agency Transition Directors Council to implement White House Council policy. The Agency Transition Directors Council is made up of representatives of the fifteen departments and transition-related agencies, and its cochairs are the federal transition coordinator and the Office of Management and Budget's deputy for management. the councils must be formed at least six months prior to a presidential election. by November 1, there should be an agreed-upon memorandum of understanding establishing the rules governing information-gathering in the departments and agencies as well as a method for settling disputes.

Gradually the time frame for a presidential transition has moved up by at least three months. Additionally, Congress and the president agreed upon an organizational structure to assist a president-elect in gathering information and having security clearances for those on their transition staff who needed them.

PRESIDENTIAL TRANSITIONS IN THE TWENTY-FIRST CENTURY: TACIT UNDERSTANDINGS AND DISCRETION IN TRANSITION IMPLEMENTATION

In addition to transition law, presidential transitions have benefitted from tacit understandings among presidents concerning the presidency as an institution. Until 2020, incumbent presidents who lost their campaigns for reelection have quickly conceded their loss and, secondly, called upon their staffs to pave a smooth road for the president-elect and his team. George H. W. Bush, our most recent one-term president who ran for reelection, instructed his White House senior staff the day following his 1992 defeat to "be helpful and leave no ticking time bombs for the incoming Clinton administration," according to his White House economic and domestic policy adviser Roger Porter.[9] "The voters have spoken, and our job is not to make the task of the incoming administration more difficult than it would otherwise be," he told his aides. In addition to providing briefings on key subjects such as the then-current Haitian boatlift crisis, Bush went beyond the requirements of the law in other ways as well.

One of the most significant actions a sitting president can take to help his successor get off to a clean start is to dismiss all of the officials he appointed to political positions. That way an incoming president can start off with his own team and not have to spend his early days firing people. Andrew Card explained how President George H. W. Bush handled the issue. Card called Warren Christopher, who was handling the transition for President Clinton and, on President Bush's instruction, asked him if they would like for Bush officials to clear out political appointees or if the Clinton team would prefer to do it when they came in. As happens with most administrations, the Clinton transition staff wanted offices cleared out with a few exceptions. "You give us the names and we'll handle it the way you tell it," Card said. He then asked for resignations or told appointees: "The President-elect is likely to want you to stay on for a while. Will you stay?"[10]

The 2008 transition is viewed as an ideal one, in part because of the tacit understandings observed on both sides that transitions make a difference to the foundation of a presidency. In late 2007, President Bush told Joshua Bolten, "Go all-out to make sure that the transition is as effective as it possibly can be, especially in the national security area."[11] To that end, Bolten took actions that brought about a smooth transition, but were not required by law:

- In summer 2008, Bolten brought into the White House representatives of the presumptive candidates, John McCain and Barack Obama.
- Bolten gave the green light to having candidates include names for FBI clearances for their agency review team members and those who would be working on the transition should they win the election.
- The representatives also worked on a required memorandum of understanding that would govern the interactions between the transition team members and the federal government.
- In order to avoid a traditional rush at the end of an administration, Bolten established time lines for department and agencies to recommend rules and regulations.
- Representatives of the Bush and Obama teams discussed the financial crisis that erupted in September 2008 as well as the possible collapse of the American auto industry.

There was nothing in transition law requiring, or even suggesting, such work, but it was important for the quality of the Obama transition into office.

The discretion presidents and their staffs have to aid an incoming team beyond the requirements of law were important in other areas of the Bush operation. In that final year of the George W. Bush administration, National Security advisor Steve Hadley also began early transition work with the preparation of memoranda detailing issues and countries important to those working in the National Security Commission in the next administration. Following the election, there were subject briefings and sessions between the incoming and outgoing members of the national security teams where, sitting side by side, the Obama officials could ask questions of their counterparts.

DISCRETIONARY PREPARATIONS APPLY TO CANDIDATES: BUSH AND BIDEN PREPARE FOR TRUNCATED TRANSITION

Discretion is also exercised by candidates, not just those in government. In the two cases where the results of the twenty-first century presidential elections were delayed, both George W. Bush and Joseph Biden prepared in advance. In both cases, it served them well. Neither the Bush nor the Biden teams of appointees, who were ready to review government materials, were allowed to access the materials department and agency officials had prepared for them nor talk to officials then serving in government. Nor could their representatives work with officials at the Office of Government Ethics. For the Biden team, the memorandum of understanding governing was by law signed by both candidates prior to the election. That meant in Biden's case that his teams would be allowed into government offices to gather materials and talk to officials there once the election was called. They did so on November 24 after the late afternoon determination the day before by GSA administrator Emily Murphy that Biden was the president-elect. In a letter to Biden, she said: "I came to my decision independently, based on the law and available facts. . . . I did not receive any direction to delay my determination." Instead, she said she reached her decision "because of recent developments involving legal challenges and certifications of election results."[12] The Associated Press, traditionally a key source in calling the winner of a presidential election, called the race on November 7, the Saturday following the November 3 election after Arizona certified Biden's win in that state.[13] He received his first President's Daily Brief on December 1. George Bush worked with a later transition time frame as the Supreme Court decision came down December 23, followed by Vice President Al Gore's concession on December 13, the day following the Supreme Court decision. David Barram ascertained Bush as the winner following the Gore concession.

George W. Bush had thirty-seven transition days before his inauguration on January 20, and Biden had fifty-seven, far from the normal approximately seventy-five days. Yet both developed several strategies that ameliorated their situations. First, both Bush and Biden had narrowed the issues they campaigned on, which led to an early focus on issues for campaigning. For Bush, education, military spending, faith-based offices, and tax cuts were campaign issues and then early presidential initiatives. Biden focused on mitigating strategies for handling the COVID-19 virus, economic recovery, and racial justice issues.

Second, Bush and Biden had similar strategies for staffing their administrations. The White House came first for both. When Biden entered office, he had 206 White House staff members appointed and ready to serve. Their choices for Joint Chiefs of Staff were people with long government and White House experience.

Third, both men had their Cabinet picks lined up before they came in, but Biden faced a slower confirmation process because of the two Georgia Senate runoff elections on January 7 that decided party control of the Senate. The Senate did not come in until January 17, which delayed the traditional preinauguration nominee hearings.

Finally, as experienced government officials, both Biden and Bush consulted the many people they knew who were familiar with departmental and agency operations. While Bush had not served in office at the national level, he knew officials through his experience with his father's presidency. Biden had served in the Senate for thirty-six years and the vice presidency for eight. He knew officials who had recently served in office. Additionally, the turnover of Trump administration officials was high, with many of those leaving willing to talk to Biden transition staff.

Using discretion to begin the transition process on their own with experienced staff worked out well for both presidents. They came into the presidency with public support for the manner in which they handled their transitions. While Bush came into office with 47.9 percent of the vote to Gore's 48.4 percent, after his early days in office, he had a Gallup job approval rating of 57 percent. Biden also had a 57 percent approval in the first Gallup poll as president.[14] Both men got off to a good start despite the delayed affirmation of their winning the presidency. Not having budget and program information was more a problem in the Trump-to-Biden transition than it was for Bush who had the cooperation of the Clinton transition team and the framework established in the executive order Clinton issued creating a Presidential Transition Coordinating Council.

THE LAW, TACIT UNDERSTANDINGS, AND DISCRETION

These three ingredients have been critical to the creation of peaceful transitions of power, even in the worst of circumstances, as was the case in 2021 when Biden took the oath of office. Chris Liddell, who in 2020 to 2021 served as cochair of the White House Transition Coordinating Council, discussed the importance of the law to his actions in preparing for the Trump transition out of office. In the lead-up to the election, Liddell's work was cited by many of the transition participants on all sides as being according to law. Liddell summed up his work: "What I tried to do was use precedent as my friend, . . . In particular, in the pre-election period, but then in the post-election period as well."[15]

The missing element in this discussion is the importance of the people who interpret and implement the law. No matter the political swirl that surrounded them, career staff in the federal government carried out the law as it has developed and been interpreted over the sixty-year period from 1962 when the first discussions of transition legislation arose.

NOTES

1. Jonathan Weisman and Annie Karni, "McConnell Denounces R.N.C. Censure of Jan. 6 Panel Members," *Washington Post*, February 6, 2022.

2. There were objections to the counts of Arizona and Pennsylvania. The objections to Arizona's vote were rejected by the Senate on a 6–93 vote and by the House with a 121–33 vote. The Pennsylvania objections were dismissed by the Senate 7–92 and by the House on a 138–282 vote.

3. Jeffrey W. Jones, "Biden Begins Term with 57% Job Approval," Gallup News, February 4, 2021, https://news.gallup.com/poll/329348/biden-begins -term-job-approval.aspx.

4. Kenneth Hechler, "Ken Hechler Oral History Interview," interview by Niel M. Johnson, Harry S. Truman Library and Museum, November 29, 1985, https://www.trumanlibrary.gov/library/oral-histories/hechler.

5. Harry Truman, "Message to Dwight D. Eisenhower Inviting Him to a Luncheon and Briefing at the White House," American Presidency Project, August 14, 1952, https://www.presidency.ucsb.edu/documents/message-dwight -d-eisenhower-inviting-him-luncheon-and-briefing-the-white-house.

6. Carl Brauer, *Presidential Transitions: Eisenhower through Reagan* (New York: Oxford University Press, 1988).

7. Executive and Legislative Reorganization Subcommittee of the Committee on Government Operations, Hearing Presidential Transition Act of 1962, H.R. 12478, at 4 (September 18, 1962).

8. Exec. Order No. 13176 (2000).

9. Roger Porter, interview with Martha Joynt Kumar, November 11, 2020.

10. Andrew Card, interview with Martha Joynt Kumar, November 11, 2020.

11. Joshua Bolten, interview with Martha Joynt Kumar, June 25, 2009.

12. Brian Naylor and Alana Wise, "President-Elect Biden to Begin Formal Transition Process after Agency OK," NPR, November 24, 2020, https://www .npr.org/sections/biden-transition-updates/2020/11/23/937956178/trump -administration-to-begin-biden-transition-protocols.

13. Deborah Riechmann and Zeke Miller, "Top Secret: Biden Gets Access to President's Daily Brief," Associated Press, December 1, 2020, https://ap news.com/article/joe-biden-receive-intelligence-briefing-d235a1e5bdc4bb 8587de5c15d2945a38.

14. Jones, "Biden Begins Term with 57% Job Approval."

15. Christopher Liddell, interview with Martha Joynt Kumar, April 20, 2021.

CHAPTER 3

Foreign Policy Interactions between Congress and the White House in the Twenty-First Century

Jonathan Burks

In the last twenty years, it has become commonplace to bemoan the decline of Congress as a deliberative body and to lament the increasingly regular deviation from "regular order." These complaints are rooted in very real changes in how Congress operates that began in earnest in 1995 with the end of forty years of continuous Democratic control of at least one house of Congress. But the complaints also reflect the changing nature and pace of communication between the electorate and its elected representatives. These dynamics have played out across the full range of political issues, including not least the formation and execution of national security policy. While the dominant narrative is of congressional decline with an ever stronger and more independent executive branch, on closer examination, the trend is less clear.

Congress has always faced impediments to being a full partner of the executive when it comes to national security. As the US Supreme Court famously observed back in 1936, the president is the "sole organ of the federal government in the field of international relations."[1] Though Congress has a stronger hand to play in creating and equipping the armed forces, the president has the innate advantages of "energy in the executive" that Alexander Hamilton characterized as "decision, activity, secrecy, and dispatch."[2]

In addition to the constitutional advantages conferred on the executive, Congress has, for an extended period, both chosen to defer to presidential leadership in national security policy and provided legal authorities that have bolstered that leadership. Many of these provisions grant the president national security authorities conditioned on the lack of disapproval of one or both houses of Congress. However, with the elimination of the legislative veto, these conditions are honored as a matter of comity.

This interbranch goodwill has become increasingly scarce in the twenty-first century. Presidents of both parties have asserted broad, independent authority to employ military force, to not implement provisions of law that they believe infringe on their constitutional prerogatives, and to act counter to expressed congressional preferences if the statutes in question provide any leeway. For example, arms sales are generally approved by the executive only after clearing an informal consultative process with Congress. But in recent years, in response to delays in clearing this informal process, the executive has pushed forward with sales through the statutory process that requires notice to Congress but not its approval.

Still, Congress has never been helpless to substantively shape national security policy. First, Congress has certain specific constitutional authorities—such as maintaining a navy, raising an army, and regulating international commerce—that ensure it a role. Second, the changing nature of the national security challenges the United States faces, where economics are increasingly important to strategic objectives, implicates policy areas where Congress has more finely tuned instruments at its disposal.

It would be fanciful to suggest that Congress sufficiently guards its institutional prerogatives in this space or that it adeptly exercises its powers, but it remains a vital partner to the executive in the formation and execution of national security policy, even in the era of the twenty-first-century presidency.

THE WARS OF THE TWENTY-FIRST CENTURY

The defining national security challenges of the twenty-first century thus far have been the wars against al-Qaeda and other Islamist extremists and the war in Iraq. These conflicts have been the primary crucible for the evolution of the relationship between Congress and the executive. While many commentators have argued that Congress has abdicated its constitutional role in the conduct of these conflicts, a more nuanced appraisal shows that Congress has been consistently and decisively engaged but in ways that respect the president's leading role in the development of strategy and the execution of operations.

Just seven days after the terrorist attacks of September 11, 2001, both houses of Congress adopted (with only one dissenting vote) the Authorization for Use of Military Force (AUMF) against al-Qaeda and its associated forces. The operative language of the AUMF is just sixty words long and provides Congress's blessing for operations against those who carried out the terrorist attack. The AUMF was the result of intensive negotiations within the executive branch and between Congress and the executive. Questions that would be revisited in future years such as how to define the target of operations and how to define the geographic scope of operations were debated directly between congressional leaders and executive branch officials. The resulting resolution is the result of those negotiations.

Over the ensuing twenty years, the AUMF would serve as the legal basis for the invasion and (failed) reconstruction efforts in Afghanistan; the raid that killed Osama bin Laden in Pakistan; countless air strikes against al-Qaeda and associated forces in Pakistan, Yemen, Somalia, Syria, and Iraq; maritime operations off the coast of Somalia; and ultimately operations against the so-called Islamic State (IS), which, having grown out of al-Qaeda, was at the time of the US operations against it engaged in open warfare against al-Qaeda. Critics point to the geographic—and strategic—sprawl of these operations, the two decades (and counting) of the conflict, and especially the war against IS as evidence that, with the Pentagon and Ground Zero still smoking and the nation grieving in shock at the murder on domestic soil of over three thousand people, Congress wrote a blank check that four presidents have used to conduct operations of their choosing. Yale law professor Oona Hathaway, for example, has argued that "there has been little democratic accountability for the many wars the United States has waged in the past seventeen years."[3]

But these arguments ignore the active role of Congress throughout this period in overseeing the conduct of the war, authorizing and funding its conduct, restructuring the federal government, and providing new tools to the executive. Criticism of a lack of congressional attention to the wars is actually an artifact of a changing media landscape and ultimately the failure of the public debate to conform to outdated notions of what public discourse around issues of war and peace looks like. For many, the frame of reference is the debate around the Vietnam War, which, at its peak, dominated the media and generated mass protests. Today, the media landscape is fragmented, and the more numerous "major" outlets very rarely align around a narrative on controversial debates. So instead of relying on media coverage to judge Congress's performance, we have to look more closely at what Congress is actually doing to assess whether it is fulfilling its national security duties.

Oversight

Oversight is one of the principal means by which Congress influences the actions of the president. While public hearings are the most visible manifestation of oversight, they are not necessarily the most important, especially in areas of national security, where classification issues can prevent fulsome public hearings. And since the advent of routine live broadcasts of hearings, they can also degenerate into playing to the cameras, where lawmakers and witnesses spend more time speaking to the broader public and less time engaging each other in a meaningful exchange of information and perspectives. A review of the hearing record of the past two decades shows that the subset of committees responsible for national security have conducted scores of hearings on the wars. But these highly visible (if not highly observed) hearings are only a fraction of the oversight Congress has conducted. There have been countless staff briefings, congressional delegation trips into the various war zones, and one-off meetings between executive branch officials and their congressional overseers. Congressional travel is sometimes derided as a boondoggle, but travel into the war zones provided members of Congress and their staffs with an opportunity to get past the administrations' talking points and hear directly from diplomats, development officials, and the people fighting the war. While the level of candor varied, repeated visits by the most diligent members of the oversight committees enabled them to develop their own appraisals of the situation. This continual engagement has shaped how executive branch officials weighed strategic choices and the consequences of action and inaction. As discussed later in this chapter, attention from congressional overseers has motivated consequential decisions.

Authorization and Funding

Congress's oversight responsibility is derivative of its legislative power.[4] While oversight is generally conducted by smaller groups of senators and representatives, legislating requires the participation of the entire body. Here, too, Congress has been active throughout the wars. Every year of the wars, Congress has adopted a National Defense Authorization Act. This omnibus legislation has often served as an occasion for Congress to debate the course and conduct of the wars. Debates over this bill (and the annual appropriations bills) have often included votes to repeal (or deny funding to implement) the AUMF or the 2002 authorization for the war in Iraq.

In addition to votes on the authority to conduct the war, Congress has also taken an active role in changing the organization, training, and equipment of the armed forces to better meet the needs of the war. This has included complex interplay between the executive branch and Congress over the relative priority of modernization of the force to face a near-peer competitor and meeting the counterinsurgency challenge arising in the present wars. Take, for examples, the service-life extension of the A-10 aircraft and the development of the mine-resistant ambush-protected (MRAP) armored vehicles, which were each the product of interactions between the Department of Defense and Congress, with Congress ultimately prioritizing the needs of the wars over modernization.

The A-10 is a ground-attack aircraft that provides combat air support to ground troops. Its relatively low speed and lack of stealth characteristics means it can only safely operate in airspace that is under near-complete US control, a condition unlikely to be obtained in a war with a future near-peer competitor. In addition, the A-10 is an aging platform with rising costs to maintain and operate. The US Air Force viewed A-10 life extension as a lower priority relative to development and acquisition of its fifth-generation fighter aircraft programs, the F-22 and the F-35, and therefore sought to retire the A-10. Congress repeatedly overruled the air force, mandating the continued operation of the A-10 as a necessary tool in the successful conduct of the war.

The MRAP program grew out of widespread concern with the casualties suffered by American service members in Iraq and Afghanistan from improvised explosive devices (IEDs). United States troops were relying on soft-skinned vehicles like the high-mobility, multipurpose, wheeled vehicle (HMMWV or Humvee) that were designed for mobility in permissive environments and thus were excessively vulnerable to IEDs. Congress worked in partnership with the secretary of defense to dedicate increased resources and to expedite the development and deployment of MRAPs over the opposition of parts of the Defense Department that viewed the vehicle as an expensive diversion from modernization priorities. The MRAP program is estimated to have saved approximately forty thousand lives during the course of the wars in Iraq and Afghanistan.[5]

In addition, Congress has consistently funded the wars through annual and supplemental appropriations. Even as the broader appropriations process has become irregular with multiple lapses (such as government shutdowns) occurring over the last two decades, Congress, both through permanent authorities and anomalies during periods of stopgap funding, has never failed to provide the money necessary to conduct the war. All told, in the past twenty years, Congress has provided over $3.4 trillion for the conduct of the wars,[6] approved through literally scores of recorded votes. In contrast, the largest federal expenditure over this time, for Social Security payments, was provided without any votes by the contemporary congresses.

Restructuring the Federal Government

Congress has also responded to the needs of the wars by engaging in extensive restructuring of the federal government. Congress initiated these changes despite initially limited enthusiasm from the executive branch. The two most significant restructurings resulted in the creation of the Department of Homeland Security (DHS) in 2002 and the creation of the Office of the Director of National Intelligence (ODNI) in 2004. Both restructurings were undertaken as a direct response to perceived weaknesses in our ability to conduct the war that became politically salient due to scrutiny driven by creations of Congress.

In the case of DHS, shortcomings in how the federal government was organized to secure the border and respond to threats to the US homeland led to a consolidation of functions from eleven cabinet departments and independent agencies and the creation of the first new cabinet department in thirteen years. Initially, the executive branch was opposed to the creation of DHS.[7] President George W. Bush ultimately became the chief proponent of establishing DHS following public scrutiny arising from congressional hearings on the 9/11 attacks. Importantly, the attention Congress directed at the shortcomings of the domestic security bureaucracy coincided with an internal executive branch initiative to develop a border security agency. Resistance from the president's Cabinet to that border security agency proposal persuaded President Bush to order the secret preparation of a more far-reaching DHS proposal. The Bush DHS proposal ultimately became a centerpiece of the 2002 congressional elections.[8] And following Republicans' surprisingly strong results, Bush and Congress reached an agreement that led to the enactment of the Department of Homeland Security Act of 2002.

The reorganization of the intelligence community, the centerpiece of which was the creation of ODNI, was the direct result of recommendations from the National Commission on Terrorist Attacks Upon the United States (or the 9/11 Commission) created by Congress "to prepare a full and complete account of the circumstances surrounding the September 11 attacks." The 9/11 Commission's moral authority was the necessary impetus for Congress to overcome resistance within the executive branch (especially from the Defense Department that houses most of the intelligence community) to the creation of ODNI.[9]

Empowering the Executive

Unlike the organizational changes that were to varying degrees forced on the executive, the executive branch actively sought enhanced authority from Congress in several areas to improve its ability to meet the terrorist threat. The Uniting and Strengthening America by Providing Appropriate Tools Required to Intercept and Obstruct Terrorism Act (or the Patriot Act) was enacted forty-five days after the September 11 attacks and significantly expanded surveillance authorities. The final act was the result of negotiations between and among the White House, the Department of Justice, the intelligence community, and multiple committees in Congress. As a result of the compromises reached in that negotiation, many authorities under the Patriot Act were provided for limited time periods. Over the last twenty years, Congress has repeatedly debated these authorities, amended them, and ultimately allowed some of them to expire in 2020.

Similarly, in the wake of judicial rulings that called into question the executive's ability to detain and try suspected terrorists in military commissions, the executive branch asked Congress to establish a statutory regime to govern the detention and trial of persons captured in the course of the war. The resulting legal regime has been the subject of public debate and rounds of legislative amendments in response to judicial rulings and executive branch policy changes. Here Congress has sought to provide the executive with the ability to detain suspected terrorists while limiting its ability to use certain interrogation techniques and to release those individuals the executive no longer believes are threats to the country.

War Strategy and Conduct

Given that the Constitution entrusts the president with the commander-in-chief power to direct the conduct of military operations, Congress is not well positioned to dictate strategy. The tools available to Congress—providing and revoking authorization, providing or denying funding—are blunt instruments that are best used as tools to force interbranch discussions but are, in the final analysis, binary and therefore often lack credibility in real-world negotiations. This can be seen, for example, in the conduct of the war in Iraq. Early US strategy in Iraq was driven, in part, by a view that US forces were an irritant that could worsen the insurgency. This belief argued for a limited troop presence and a force posture that kept American forces separate from the Iraqi population. Even as many in Congress became increasingly concerned about the deterioration of security conditions in Iraq and the seeming futility of US operations there, Congress was unable to force a change in strategy, perhaps revealing that the upper hand in foreign policy remains with the executive. While the congressionally created Iraq Study Group and criticism from members of Congress played a role in driving the public mood on the war, it was ultimately long-running internal administration deliberations and the dismissal of defense secretary Donald Rumsfeld that led to the adoption of a counterinsurgency strategy that posited that more, and more active, US forces were essential in order to deny the insurgents access to the Iraqi population. This change in strategy came to be known as "the Surge."[10]

Another example of this relative congressional weakness is the war in Libya. President Barack Obama's decision to intervene militarily in support of rebels fighting to overthrow Libyan dictator Muammar Gaddafi was taken without congressional authorization and continued in the face of explicit congressional opposition in the form of a nonbinding, bipartisan House resolution calling for the withdrawal of the United States military from the air and naval operations in and around Libya.[11]

While this resolution was intended to forestall passage of an ostensibly binding resolution, the fact that Congress chose not to exercise its ultimate power demonstrates its reticence to impose its policy preferences decisively on questions of military strategy and operations.

However, in those areas where Congress's tools are more variated— for example, the levels and uses of appropriations, the structure of the executive branch, the legal authorities available to the executive— Congress has been quite active. Moreover, the nature of the dialogue between Congress and the executive is not as one-sided as often assumed. Congress has acted decisively, both in putting items on the agenda (such as intelligence reform) and in deciding controversial issues over the objections of the executive (such as the A-10 life extension discussed previously).

INTERNATIONAL ECONOMIC POLICY

While the wars have been the most important foreign policy events of the last twenty years, they are not the totality of America's national security policy. In recent years, international economic policy has taken on greater importance, especially as the foreign policy establishment shifts focus to great power competition with China (and to a lesser degree Russia). In these important areas, Congress has significantly shaped US policy, both in action and inaction, with specific key areas.

Trade Policy

Since the Second World War, US trade policy has been premised on the idea that with respect to any particular trade agreement, Congress is likely to be dominated by the parochial interests of those who stand to lose from increased competition from abroad. Therefore, successive Congresses that favored trade liberalization as a general proposition established mechanisms—principally trade promotion authority (TPA)—to facilitate executive branch–led trade liberalization while limiting congressional discretion. These mechanisms were often accompanied by discretionary authority for the executive to unilaterally take action to prevent adverse consequences from trade liberalization.

The most important moments of congressional engagement on trade, therefore, became periodic votes to renew TPA and the subsequent up-or-down votes on the legislation to implement the resulting trade liberalization agreements. This pattern held for much of the period under discussion, with two votes to renew TPA (in 2002 and 2015) and eleven votes to approve trade-liberalizing agreements.

Trade policy was generally seen as principally an economic policy question rather than a foreign policy one. This changed with the election of President Donald Trump in 2016. Having run on a promise to fix America's "horrible and unfair trade deals" and to stop China's "rape" of the United States, trade policy was increasingly viewed as a foreign policy issue.[12] Once in office, the national security strategy issued by President Trump made the geopolitical importance of trade explicit, declaring that "China [is] determined to make economies less free and less fair."[13]

Using trade laws that had been written on the assumption of a generally pro-free-trade executive, President Trump initiated trade wars with China, the European Union, Canada, Mexico, and others. He did so by invoking existing trade laws with disputed applicability to the problems he sought to address. While few questioned the applicability of Section 301 authorities (relating to unfair trade practices) as a response to intellectual property theft by China, the invocation of Section 232 authorities (relating to national security threats arising from trade) against treaty allies in North America and Europe was arguably inappropriate.[14]

The traditionally pro-trade policy leaders in Congress on the US Senate Committee on Finance and House Committee on Ways and Means opposed many of these exercises of executive power. Congress as an institution, however, proved unable or unwilling to exercise its plenary authority to limit the executive in this space. Moreover, when presented with the United States–Mexico–Canada trade agreement, which was more protectionist than the North American Free Trade Agreement (NAFTA) that it was replacing,[15] Congress rapidly approved the agreement with a larger bipartisan majority than has been typical of prior free-trade agreements. With the assumptions about relative support for liberalizing trade reversed, the mechanisms that Congress created to limit its own protectionist tendencies over three quarters of a century are now producing more protectionist results than originally intended.

Controlling Sensitive Technology

Congress has been somewhat more effective in playing an active role with respect to controls on sensitive technology. In 2006, a controversy erupted over the proposed sale of port management rights for six major US ports to a firm based in the United Arab Emirates. The sale was ultimately scuttled by the business parties in response to political pressures. Of more lasting consequence, though, were the resulting reforms of the US government's process for reviewing investment from foreign persons in the US economy. Congress, despite opposition from the executive branch, passed the Foreign Investment and National Security Act of 2007, which, for the first time, codified the Committee on Foreign Investment in the United States (CFIUS). These reforms were revisited in 2018 in the Foreign Investment Risk Review Modernization Act of 2018, which further tightened US investment policy and significantly broadened the scope of national security reviews of inbound investment. In both cases, Congress acted to establish rules different than those that the executive branch left to its own devices would have chosen. In the former case, Congress was more restrictive with respect to investment and in the latter more liberal.

For the first time since 1979, Congress also passed a comprehensive reauthorization of the rules governing export of sensitive technologies. The export control regime had operated under emergency presidential authority since 2001. By taking this action, Congress reclaimed authority from the executive and exercised independent judgment on the appropriate policy in this space.

Sanctions and Other Restrictions

A similar pattern holds with respect to increasing congressional assertiveness when it comes to sanctions and other kinds of restrictive economic policies. In 2017, Congress passed the Countering America's Adversaries Through Sanctions Act, which limited presidential discretion to not apply sanctions against Iran, North Korea, and Russia in certain circumstances. While President Trump complained that the law unconstitutionally limited his flexibility in the conduct of US foreign policy, he and his administration abided by the law.[16]

Furthermore, in 2020 and 2021, Congress passed the Holding Foreign Companies Accountable Act and the Uyghur Forced Labor Prevention Act. The Holding Foreign Companies Accountable Act closes a loophole in US securities laws that allowed foreign companies (mainly Chinese companies) to trade on US stock exchanges even though their auditors were not subject to inspection by the US auditing regulator. Given bipartisan congressional concern about surreptitious Chinese Communist Party control of Chinese companies, the bill speaks to Congress's belief that Americans need to have confidence that Chinese companies are subject to the same standards for transparency as any other publicly traded company.

Long-standing US law excludes any goods made with forced labor from being imported. On a case-by-case basis, Customs and Border Protection has excluded goods suspected of being made with forced labor in China's Xinjiang province. The Uyghur Forced Labor Prevention Act creates a presumption that any imports from Xinjiang are the result of forced labor. These are only the most recent examples of Congress reshaping high-profile aspects of the economic relationship with China.

Organizational Reform

Congress has also taken a hand in restructuring the executive branch to better meet the needs of great power competition. Working in partnership with the Trump administration to provide a more flexible and capable tool for economic competition with China in third-world countries, Congress created the International Development Finance Corporation to facilitate projects in middle- and low-income countries. Congress also formed the US Agency for Global Media to better direct US efforts "to inform, engage and connect people around the world in support of freedom and democracy."[17]

Overall, the willingness and ability of Congress to act in the international economic space seems to be growing. Even in the trade policy space where Congress has been less assertive of its traditional policy views, the Biden administration's continuation of Trump-era trade policies suggests that the trade policy posture may simply reflect prevailing political and policy views.

CONCLUSION

The pattern that emerges from this review of congressional engagement in national security policy is not straightforward. Congress has acted repeatedly and decisively on many of the key issues facing the country in this space. But it has done so in a way that is somehow unsatisfying for many observers of Congress. There is a feeling among the commentariat that Congress has paid too little attention and that it has given free rein to the executive branch.

In part, this sentiment reflects the changing manner in which Congress does its job. With the introductions of cameras onto the floors of both houses and into the hearing rooms of most of the committees, more of the real deliberations of Congress have moved behind closed doors. As discussed, instead of being used to elicit information, hearings are often now opportunities to give speeches. And instead of relying on daily media reports, constituents are now able to observe in real time whether their member of Congress is compromising with their political rivals or is holding firm to the party line. So-called sunshine laws have thus had the unintended result of increased formal transparency but practical policy opacity.

However, it's not just a question of Congress doing its work more opaquely. There has also been a decline in the informal exercise of congressional power. The inability of Congress to regularly enact appropriations and authorization bills individually and on schedule has reduced the executive branch's responsiveness to the sentiment of Congress. Increasingly, the executive recognizes that Congress is unlikely to exercise its hard powers in legislation, and thus there's little reason to heed its soft power as expressed by individual members in committee hearings, letters, and report language. The notable exception to this trend has been the regular enactment of the defense authorization bills, which not coincidentally is also the area where Congress retains its most effective working relationship with the executive branch.

Ultimately, however, those who look to Congress to dominate policymaking in national security policy are bound to be disappointed. Going back to Hamilton's observation, the plural nature of Congress will always limit its ability to act with dispatch and direction. Instead, there will always be fits and starts.

NOTES

1. United States v. Curtiss-Wright Export Corp., 299 U.S. 304 (1936), https://supreme.justia.com/cases/federal/us/299/304/.

2. Alexander Hamilton, "The Federalist No. 70 [15 March 1788]," Founders Online, accessed July 22, 2023, https://founders.archives.gov/documents/Hamilton/01-04-02-0221.

3. Oona Hathaway, "How to Revive Congress's War Powers," Texas National Security Review, November 2019, https://tnsr.org/roundtable/policy-roundtable-the-war-powers-resolution/.

4. McGrain v. Daugherty, 273 U.S. 135 (1927), https://supreme.justia.com/cases/federal/us/273/135/#tab-opinion-1931647.

5. "Mine-Resistant, Ambush-Protected (MRAP) Vehicles: Background and Issues for Congress," Congressional Research Service, August 10, 2011, https://crsreports.congress.gov/product/pdf/RS/RS22707.

6. Neta C. Crawford, "The U.S. Budgetary Costs of the Post-9/11 Wars," Watson Institute of International and Public Affairs, September 1, 2021, https://watson.brown.edu/costsofwar/files/cow/imce/papers/2021/Costs%20of%20War_U.S.%20Budgetary%20Costs%20of%20Post-9%2011%20Wars_9.1.21.pdf.

7. "Homeland Department Created," CQ Almanac, 2003, http://library.cqpress.com/cqalmanac/cqal02–236–10378–664466.

8. Kenneth F. Warren, ed., *Encyclopedia of U.S. Campaigns, Election, and Electoral Behavior* (Newbury Park, CA: Sage, 2008), 304–305.

9. Michael Allen, *Blinking Red: Crisis and Compromise in American Intelligence After 9/11* (Williamsport, MD: Potomac Books, 2013).

10. George W. Bush, *Decision Points* (New York: Crown, 2010).

11. H.R. Res. 292, 112th Cong. (June 3, 2011).

12. Donald J. Trump, "Republican Nomination Acceptance Speech," July 19, 2016, https://assets.donaldjtrump.com/DJT_Acceptance_Speech.pdf; Nick Glass, "Trump: 'We can't continue to allow China to rape our country,'" *Politico*, 2016, https://www.politico.com/blogs/2016-gop-primary-live-updates-and-results/2016/05/trump-china-rape-america-222689.

13. *National Security Strategy of the United States of America* (Washington, DC: White House, 2017), https://trumpwhitehouse.archives.gov/wp-content/uploads/2017/12/NSS-Final-12–18–2017–0905.pdf.

14. Scott Lincicome and Inu Manak, "Protectionism or National Security? The Use and Abuse of Section 232," Cato Institute, March 9, 2021, https://www.cato.org/policy-analysis/protectionism-or-national-security-use-abuse-section-232.

15. Mary E. Lovely and Jeffery J. Schott, "The USMCA: New, Modestly Improved, but Still Costly," Peterson Institute for International Economics, December 17, 2019, https://www.piie.com/blogs/trade-and-investment-policy-watch/usmca-new-modestly-improved-still-costly.

16. "Statement by President Donald J. Trump on the Signing of H.R. 3364," White House, August 2, 2017, https://trumpwhitehouse.archives.gov/briefings-statements/statement-president-donald-j-trump-signing-h-r-3364/.

17. "Home," US Agency for Global Media, accessed September 19, 2023, https://www.usagm.gov/who-we-are/mission/#:~:text=The%20mission%20of%20United%20States,support%20of%20freedom%20and%20democracy.

PANEL ONE

The Management of the Evolving Twenty-First-Century Presidency

Edited version of a conversation at the February 15, 2022, Bipartisan Policy Center conference focusing on how the presidency is run.

Jason Grumet, former president, Bipartisan Policy Center: The Bipartisan Policy Center focuses on durable national policy that we believe requires the engagement across a broad ideological spectrum. And as a result, we normally focus most of our attention on the Congress. It has occurred to us that the Congress is a somewhat less dynamic, vibrant, efficient enterprise than it once was. And in that vacuum, the presidency, the executive branch, has absconded with significant amounts of effective national power. If you think back to President Clinton and the Mexican peso crisis, he was flexing some executive muscle. President Bush, post-9/11 as a wartime president with a little bit of whispering in his ear from Vice President Cheney, announced a rather expanded imagination of presidential power. President Obama's pen-and-pad strategy and proliferation of executive orders followed by President Trump's "I alone can fix it" [rhetoric are] somewhat unique imagination[s] of the role of the presidency. And now President Biden, for whom I think the story gets mixed, right? There's been a strong emphasis around federal authority on mandates, around vaccines and public-health urgency, and at the same time a pretty deferential approach to Congress on a bunch of priorities.

The Bipartisan Policy Center's new initiative on the study of American presidential leadership is the perfect venue to look at these questions. The Presidential Leadership Initiative is led by Dr. Tevi Troy. Dr. Troy is a classically trained presidential historian and yet, despite that knowledge, actually went to work as a senior official in the White House. So, he brings both a little bit of a historic framework and also some practical experience to this discussion. He's admired on both sides of the aisle. He's also a creative and prolific writer. What is unique about Tevi and the kind of DC literary scene is he writes books that are actually not about himself, which adds to the national understanding and appreciation of really the past, the present, and the future of our democracy.

* * *

Tevi Troy, director of the Presidential Leadership Initiative, Bipartisan Policy Center: The four presidents of the twenty-first century so far have changed the presidency in significant ways, which is really important, because the presidency is a common touchstone, the most senior executive in our nation, and really an essential player in our system if we are going to make it through the many challenges that we as a nation face. And so, if you look at the last twenty years, you would start with George W. Bush, for whom I worked, and he is faced with the crisis after 9/11.

And what he does is he create[s] and expand[s] a Homeland Security state that didn't really exist beforehand. He also is somewhat aggressive in his use of signing statements in a way that often alienated the Democratic members of Congress. And the signing statements allowed the presidency to put its stamp on pieces of legislation that are passed by Congress in a way that the legislative branch didn't always necessarily like. Bush is succeeded by Barack Obama, who has some legislative success in his first year but then is stymied after the Republicans take Congress. And Obama then looks more to executive power throughout the rest of his presidency. David Letterman had a joke in Obama's second term that Obama goes to the doctor and is told that he passes his physical and then Letterman says [it] is a good thing because it's the first time he's passed something in years. So, Obama really can't get things through Congress. He then engages in this pen-and-phone presidency where he actually does [actions] through executive order, things that he said previously were unconstitutional for him to do via executive actions, such as the DREAMer's action that he took in November of 2014. And then you have Donald Trump who wanted to see what he could do unilaterally as president, as opposed to working necessarily through the levers of government. And now we have Joe Biden as president. And what we've seen is Biden is very ambitious legislatively and trying to do a kind of FDR- or LBJ-type agenda at a time when he has much narrower congressional majorities than either of those two. In fact, he has a fifty-fifty tie in the Senate.

So those four people who've held the presidency have really changed things. Individually, each of those changes is significant and worth noting. But in toto, I think we are now in a situation where the presidency that Joe Biden now inhabits is vastly different from the presidency that Bill Clinton passed on to George W. Bush at the end of the twentieth century.

What does this mean for our nation? What are the parameters of how the presidency has changed? And how, if we want, can we fix it? Should we change things? Are we on an inevitable trajectory or is there a chance that things might change? Can political leadership, can individual leaders say we want to go in a different direction? What would that different direction look like?

* * *

Jonathan Burks, former chief of staff to Speaker of the House Paul Ryan: If power is accruing to the presidency, it must be coming from someplace. And so, we look at the Congress as a lens for clarifying what's changed and what's constant in that presidential relationship. Foreign policymaking is where the president's power is at its apex. And how Congress plays in that space tells you a lot about what works and what doesn't work or what's changed and what hasn't changed in terms of the presidential power and inner branch. So, when you look at the details of the last twenty years and what's occurred on foreign policy, what's in the national security space, it's a lot more nuanced picture than sort of the standard narrative of the presidency is up and the Congress is down. There are one or two axes we should be looking at that call into question the standard narrative.

One is along the axis of constitutional powers, which the constitution specifically entrusts to Congress and the president is unable to do independently—things like raising an army, maintaining a navy, raising the funds needed to conduct the wars. And that's an area where Congress has been very active and the Congress's interventions have been decisive in shaping how the executive has acted through a variety of tools that they have. The second axis that has been important is in terms of international commerce, where trade and export controls and other import restrictions and all the rest have been incredibly important tools—increasingly important tools—in foreign policy. And where there, again, the presidency has a fair bit of discretion that Congress has given it, but Congress has been very active over the last twenty years in exercising authority. And so, as we look back over the last twenty years of foreign policymaking, it's actually a complex story that shows that there are both broad areas of discretion, but there's an active Congress that limits that discretion and that provides new tools or new authorities or at times has pulled those authorities back in a way that reflects the Congress's constitutional role. Looking forward, we see that the foreign policy agenda is moving, frankly, in the direction of Congress's powers and where Congress is most adept, given the focus of the great power competition with China and Russia. One, the competition with China is very much driven by the international economic competition, where again, Congress's authorities are plenary and where the ability of the president to act without Congress is limited and somewhat clumsy. And then the second aspect of competition really is deterrence, which really relies in large measure on the shape and funding capabilities of our military, which again is critically dependent on acts of Congress and the active involvement of Congress. And so, while there's no question that the presidency has changed over the last twenty years, it's important not to overstate the case in terms of the change [that] necessarily made the presidency imperial and powerful. There are still very important checks in Congress's hands, and Congress is still exercising that authority and that ability to check presidential power.

* * *

Martha Joynt Kumar, Towson University: It's worth looking at the presidential transitions from the period of after World War II, when Harry Truman was the first president to be very concerned about a transition, through the end of the twentieth century. Transitions in that period were not particularly acrimonious, but when you look in the twenty-first century at the four presidents who come in, two of the four had truncated transitions that were delayed because of disputes in the courts—and then also with 2020, with the administrator of the General Services Administration not declaring the ascertainment of Biden's win. So that George Bush had thirty-seven days instead of the normal seventy-five or so, and Biden had only fifty-seven days. You look at the 2016 transition—that was chaotic in its own way as Donald Trump fired the staff that had worked through the transition process up to the election and then replaced it with a team led by Vice President Elect Pence, and then . . . with family members and people who had worked on the campaign, most of whom did not have government experience. The one transition that was smooth in that time period was the transition in 2008 between Bush and Obama. Bush felt that with two wars that he wanted to make sure that they had an early start and took the transition very seriously.

And Bush began his transition talking to his chief of staff, Josh Bolten, in December of 2007. And Steve Hadley, who was the national security advisor around the same time, began gathering information on memoranda on countries and issues to provide to whomever came in. And so, when you look at the series of transitions that, even though you're going to have a lot of turmoil, at the same time, when you look at Biden's transition, how was it that he was able to come in with a White House staff of 206 . . . filling out a lot of the presidential appointee positions that did not require Senate confirmation? Bush did much the same thing. And so the Biden people had their policies ready to start. And how was it that they were able to do that even if they had a shortened transition? And the same thing was true with Bush, with only thirty-seven days, [he] had his first months mapped out—first week education, second week Office of Faith-Based Initiatives in the government.

What I look at are three particular elements of transitions that have developed over time. The first is the law. Starting in 1963, you have the beginnings of transition law where the responsibility for funding transitions moves from political parties to the government itself. And it first is a matter of resources—office space and whatever needs to come with that. And then gradually there's a framework that's built where you have the White House Transition Coordinating Council that is going to develop policy. Clinton created one by executive order. And then you have the development of the Agency Transition Directors Council, which takes the policies that are established by the White House Policy Councils.

And then with representatives of all the departments and the largest agencies, then they implement the policy. There are target dates that have been put in as you've had further development of transitions, so that a president has to create these councils by six months before the election. And . . . it doesn't say who is on it, but the president still gets to decide that. And this past election [2020] was the first time that you had a sitting president who had to create a council, even though he was running for reelection. And before that, it really was an optional item, but it wasn't in 2020, which was very important for how the transition worked. And in addition to law, you have tacit understanding. So, there've been tacit understandings among presidents that have guided the actions of those in office, even when they lost reelection. While that was not true of Donald Trump, it was true of Jimmy Carter and George H. W. Bush, both of whom told their staffs that they wanted a smooth transition and to begin to work quickly, which they did. Now in this past transition, though, we did not have that from the president. The president instead refused to concede the election and then also chose to delegitimize President Biden. But even though he was doing that still, you had people in his administration who were carrying out of the law, particularly Chris Liddell, who was the deputy chief of staff who had worked on [Mitt] Romney's transition, the early transition work in 2012. And he knew transitions and followed the law. Then you have discretion. The third element is discretion, and that is the discretion that the president and whomever he appoints to run his transition, that they have to do early work if they want to.

And that was the case with George W. Bush and his chief of staff Josh Bolten, who ran that transition. Bolten took a lot of early actions, such as bringing in the representatives of the presumptive candidates, [John] McCain and Obama, bringing them in, in midsummer before the party conventions, because the party conventions were late to discuss some important issues, like the memorandum of understanding that has to be created for agency review teams to go into the departments and agencies—kind of the rules of the road for that. And then you also have, in addition to discretion that the president and his staff have, you also have discretion by candidates. Do candidates decide that they are going to spend time preparing? And in the case of Biden and George W. Bush, both of them did a lot of preparatory work. And Biden's case obviously to get to 206 people in the White House, it was a lot of personnel work. Then [there was] a decision to focus on presidential appointees who did not require Senate confirmation. He also worked on developing information and strategies on issues that may come up, . . . [that] went under a heading of unconventional challenges—what unconventional challenges could they possibly face—and then assigning people to work on those challenges, flesh them out, and then develop mitigating strategies. So, the preparatory work early is not just mandated by the government. It's also good practice by the candidates.

* * *

Tevi Troy: The candidates and the government have put so much more resources and attention into transitions in this twenty-first century. And yet the transitions have, for the most part, been less smooth, which is a paradox that is worth exploring.

* * *

Elaine Kamarck, Brookings Institution scholar and former Bill Clinton aide: I have a very straightforward proposition about the presidency, but it involves looking at the structure of the modern presidency in a new way. My argument is pretty simple: when presidents suffer implementation failures, when things go wrong that the government has some role in, it really takes a toll on the presidency. And it takes a toll on the public's perception of presidential competence. Presidents lose political capital when the government they run encounters major implementation failures. This happened to George W. Bush after Hurricane Katrina. It happened to Barack Obama after the failure of the health-care websites. It happened to Donald Trump as he tried to navigate the COVID epidemic. And it has once more happened to Joe Biden in the wake of the withdrawal from Afghanistan. In each instance, the political capital lost is nearly impossible to get back. And that's very important. For first-term presidents, implementation failures are major contributors to electoral failures. For second-term presidents, implementation failures eat up so much political capital that these presidents are hobbled in their ability to enact the major changes that they sought, that they think [are] going to be part of their legacy. So, let's start with George W. Bush. As we all remember, after Hurricane Katrina, FEMA [the Federal Emergency Management Agency] basically was a mess. And so, it was New Orleans, and the headlines read that we looked like a third-world country, which we did in the inability to help people with all the resources—all the planes, trains, and automobiles that we have in the US military—we couldn't help people for days and even months. That took a toll on Bush's second term. He had gone into the second term with, this time, a clean mandate. He had actually won the election clearly, unlike four years before. And he had big plans on Social Security reform. The

White House had set up this whole operation. And if you look at what happened to George W. Bush and his presidency, basically after that, he couldn't do anything. He basically was unable to have the political capital to make anything happen. Obama, in his second term, gets to implement his pride and joy, the Affordable Care Act. And what happens is that all the websites crash, there are hundreds of thousands of Americans trying to buy health care. And everybody is saying, "What is wrong with this government?" They can't even do what Amazon does so easily every single day.

Obviously, when we get to Trump, he was in pretty good shape until COVID hit. He had a pretty good situation, as controversial as his presidency was; the economy was really quite strong. So, when we get to Trump, what we see is a series of really awful missteps in the handling of the pandemic—missteps that were evident to everybody. The whole country was at home in 2020 while Trump was on television every day, contradicting himself, confusing things, contradicting the experts, and finally sort of giving up and giving it to the governors. That was a major implementation failure from which he did not recover. And then we come to Biden. Biden had a really very good first five months, six months of his presidency. The pandemic seemed to be going in the right direction. The chaos that seemed to characterize Trump's handling of the pandemic was gone. He passed a great big relief bill, et cetera. And then suddenly . . . the entire month of August is devoted to these horrific scenes out of Afghanistan. And while people agreed with the policy, they thought, for sure, yes, we should be out of Afghanistan. The fact of the matter was that this looked like a mess, like a screwed-up mess that hadn't been well-planned and certainly hadn't been well executed. It's damaging to these presidents because in fact, ultimately, the American people, regardless of their ideologies and all the polarization, they expect some competence from the president. They do not differentiate between the bureaucracy and everybody who works for the president and the president himself. They expect competence out of the presidency. The reason I think understanding this is important is that in the modern presidency, the emphasis and the staffing has all gone to people with communications backgrounds, not operations backgrounds.

Operations—you can find that [in] the third or the fourth tier of a White House. Communications—you find that [in] the first tier of a White House. And that's got terrible consequences because in each one of the implementation failures that I talk about . . . , there is no speech that gets you out of the hole. There isn't a speech. There isn't an ad. There isn't a communications trick that is going to restore presidential popularity and therefore presidential political capital. And I do believe that this is a reflection of the way we've set up the modern presidency, where we value communications to the detriment of operations.

* * *

Alan Rechtschaffen, trustee, Wilson Center: We ask the president to do more and more. And the more we ask the president to do, the more likelihood there is some kind of catastrophic implementation failure. Instead of focusing on the evolution created by four presidents, might it not be a legitimate thesis to look at the question of whether the presidency is a product of personality and less intrinsic power or policy?

* * *

Martha Joynt Kumar: I look at it as a product rather than personality—although clearly that's involved—but a product of their experiences. People who have been governors, for example, have tended to be decisive right from the start, where they're used to being an executive. Say, for example, I had an interview with Gerald Ford a number of years ago and asked him how he made the transition from a legislator to an executive. As a legislator, in a leadership position, he was interested in reaching consensus, and success for him was consensus. And you can see that in Biden, that that's what he's used to. If you can get everybody together, that's what you should do. Ford said that he wasn't sure how it happened, but he knew when it happened. He said one day that he was listening to a group of members of Congress, and he said to himself, "If I were in their position, I'd be saying exactly the same thing, but I'm not. And I'm making the decision." If you look at Trump, what was Trump's experience? He didn't have government elective experience. He didn't have military experience. His experience was with a family-owned business where he was not responsible to anybody other than the family. And so, he liked to control information, make the decisions himself in talking about his communications. Why did he need a press secretary? He was the one who controlled his own communications. And I think if you look at governors, through a period of time, you see how they've been decisive and also good communicators, whether it's a Woodrow Wilson who was interested in communications as a way to educate the public, Theodore Roosevelt, Franklin Roosevelt, Ronald Reagan—they all had a good sense of what leadership was about and had practiced it before they came to the presidency.

* * *

Elaine Kamarck: Well, there's no doubt that personality is important. But what has happened to our modern presidents is that the way they are chosen [has] changed fundamentally. They are chosen in the system of primaries, where what is valuable is your ability to communicate and your ability to get attention and your ability to promise things to be out there. And what is less valuable than it used to be in the old days is who you are, and what you've done, and whether you've had experience running something, governing, legislating, whatever. And we're just beginning to see the real effects of this transition we've gone through in American history, from nominations that were closed and essentially by party people to nominations that are just open. One of the features of our modern nomination systems is that we have people in there who have absolutely no business being president running for president of the United States—spiritual advisors, pizza entrepreneurs.

There are always people in each party who are in this to sell books or get themselves a spot on CNN and not because they know anything at all about governing. And I think that the emphasis on communications starts in the primaries, and you win the primaries on the basis of your ability to communicate. Then you get in the White House and what happens? Oh, there's a whole government out there. Sometimes it works, and sometimes it doesn't. And I have quotes in a book I wrote about this from people in the Obama White House who felt put upon because this website—they weren't supposed to code the websites. Other people were supposed to write code, right? And yet they were taking the brunt of this. They were taking the hit. And that's what happens in all of these failures. The White House gets very, very defensive, because the fact of the matter is that the White House has no idea . . . how things are actually operating out there. We've had four presidents now who are less experienced, with the exception of Biden, but certainly less experienced than any other presidents, and Biden is less experienced in executive management. He was never in executive management. He was a creature of the United States Senate. So, we've got a system which generates a different kind of person getting nominated and therefore elected.

Let me just end with a little story for you to think about. In 1959 to '60, Jack Kennedy had to get the approval of the governor of Pennsylvania who controlled the delegates . . . to the Democratic convention. And there were a lot from Pennsylvania. And that involved some old-fashioned smoke-filled rooms, I'm sure, and some brown liquid, I'm sure, and it involved some heavy-duty discussions about power, politics, and government. Now imagine if, in 2016, Donald Trump had had to negotiate with a powerful governor for delegates to a Democratic convention. And he went in there and he said, "I'm going to build a wall and I'm going to get Mexico to pay for it." Now we all know that's one of the dumbest statements anybody has ever made, but no one called Donald Trump on it, right? Every once in a while, a journalist would try to call him on it. But it was clearly a statement that was misleading. That was inaccurate. There was absolutely no way we were going to make Mexico pay for a wall unless we were willing to invade Mexico and steal their treasury. I mean, it was just plain out. Now, imagine if he had had to go through a gauntlet of people who knew something about governing. Basically, we are nominating people who are very good talkers, not experienced in operations. They get into the White House, and they think they can talk themselves out of these failures. And the bottom line is they can't, and it takes down their presidency.

* * *

Jonathan Burks: I thought you ought to name your paper "The Aaron Sorkin Effect." So, a lot of it—the walk and talk through the halls of the White House—will solve anything.

* * *

Elaine Kamarck: What we don't have anymore is peer review. No one who actually knows what the business is has a voice in who the nominee is—we don't. When we go to have a neurosurgeon for brain surgery, we don't ask if he's the most popular one. We ask if this person has been stamped the stamp of approval by other neurosurgeons. And we accept peer review in every part of our economy in our society, except in politics.

* * *

Tom Kahn, former House Budget Committee staff director: Arthur Schlesinger wrote his famous book *The Imperial Presidency* as a critique of the Nixon administration. But it almost seems as if that . . . was premature, that he was talking about the imperial presidency in the seventies, and maybe it's the imperial presidency that now exists in the twenty-first century. Can we adopt some of Schlesinger's concept of the imperial presidency into what this twenty-first-century presidency is?

* * *

Martha Joynt Kumar: I think the expectations of what a president can produce is very different than what he actually can produce. There are so many forces now that he has to contend with that, say, even in Arthur Schlesinger['s time] . . . he didn't. Look at the array of interest groups that exist, that have blossomed since that time, that make it difficult to write certain kinds of legislation like tax legislation. You have so many even foreign governments hiring the lobbying firms, and many of them, many firms for one country, to deal with legislation on the Hill. And the president has party members who don't owe him anything. They got there on their own, and he's just one of the voices that they listened to. So, he can come in with great expectations of what he can do and what he wants to do—tackling the virus, for example. Who would have thought that here we have a vaccine, but these are large numbers of people who are refusing to take it? And that's something that's been very important, in [terms of] Biden's difficulties with the virus. The expectations of what a president can do far outstrip what he actually can do.

Let me just take off a little bit on the government itself. When you have a government as big as the US federal government, something is going really right. And something is going really wrong all the time. There are agencies that are ready to blow up and cause you problems you didn't imagine, like the Veterans Administration health scandal that so embarrassed the Obama administration. And yet there are also great capacities in the federal government. George W. Bush could have avoided a lot of the problems he ran into in Iraq with a little bit closer attention to what the spies at the State Department were saying, as opposed to the spies at the Defense Department. And that's a long story, but it's a good one. And what happens with these modern presidents who get there by virtue of their golden tongue and their ability to talk and connect, which is important, is that they don't have any idea what's going on out there in the government they're running.

So, not only do they not know what's going to blow up in their faces, they also don't know the tools that they have so that when something happens, they can actually manage it and deal with it. I was stunned in those early months of 2020, how long it took for Donald Trump to discover the Defense Production Act. And you could actually see him on television, sort-of talking about it in a way that those of us who've been professors, we have a sixth sense for this, when your student suddenly has learned something brand new and they're trying to try it out. And that's what he was doing with the Defense Production Act. That was something he just really should've known about. So, there's a lot of operational talent that these modern presidents don't have and that they need to have or they need to somehow build into their White House.

* * *

Tevi Troy: Jonathan Burks, you worked on a transition. Do you agree with Martha on how the transitions have changed and how much were you aware of the history of transitions when you were doing the work with the transition that you did?

* * *

Jonathan Burks: There's an important element that we would be remiss to leave out, which is that much of the accretion of power to the executive hasn't been seized by the executive as much as it's been given by Congress. And so there's a series of statutes that were passed in the seventies. Many of them intended to ratchet-down the president's authority that subsequently have been sort-of reinterpreted and used in ways unintended to really give him a very broad mandate. So, I think to the degree that one worries about excessive executive power, that the first place to start is for Congress to go back and look at many of their statutes. In terms of presidential transitions, when we were working on the 2012 Romney transition that never was, I certainly was aware of the recent history. I couldn't have given you the chapter and verse back to the Truman years, which I thought were fascinating. But the challenge that we had faced coming in 2001 into the Bush administration and the contrasts with the emphasis that President Bush had placed in 2008 to 2009 on ensuring a smooth transition out of office meant that there was a lot of energy in the Romney campaign in making sure that we were doing it right, engaging together with the Obama team, who, to their credit, were engaging in good faith with their responsibilities to make the transition work.

* * *

Tevi Troy: Elaine Kamarck worked with Bill Clinton and the Clinton White House. Do you agree with this thesis that the presidency that Bill Clinton inhabited is very different than the presidency that Joe Biden now inhabits, that if you perhaps had been with Clinton and he had this level of power, maybe he would have done different things, more things, additional things? Is it sort of a wistful moment: "Wow, if we'd had this kind of power, we would have done a lot more"?

* * *

Elaine Kamarck: I think it is a different moment. I think the polarization . . . appeared during the Clinton presidency, because let's face it, in 1994, when Newt Gingrich took over the Congress, that was really the first indication that politics was going to be very different than it had been. But still, Bill Clinton was able to manage some things with Gingrich, even though the rhetoric took a definite step up in 1994. And now we're in this situation where the polarization pervades everything, including whether or not you're going to take a vaccine. Who would have thought that getting a vaccine would become a partisan issue? That's something that's sort of unbelievable to those of us who've lived long enough to see different phases of policy go forward. And during the campaign, reporters used to ask me, "Well, do you really think that Joe Biden can overcome the polarization in the Congress and in the country?" And I would give the response that I think is still true, which is, "If anybody could have done it, it would have been Joe Biden, but that's a big if." I think nobody can do it right now. I think we're in a very, very serious place. And a president for this era needs to be able to do everything right and that includes *implement*. And that's where I think the Biden's administration's first year fell down. Now they have three more years to make up. They concentrated so much on passing bills because it's who Joe Biden was. He was the legislator. So that's what he wanted to do. And that's how he measured success. And I think that my point is success is actually simple: don't screw up. And when you have a big problem, use the government to fix it as opposed to not knowing even how and where in the government to fix it. So, at this point in history, any president has a really tough road. Joe Biden's is much tougher because he has had his first implementation failure. Hopefully, for his sake, he won't have any more, and he might be able to end up with a successful first term.

* * *

Tevi Troy: How much has the presidency been changed by the increased use of the filibuster in the Senate? And part of the premise of this whole conference is this idea that Congress has ceded powers because of its inability to legislate. And in that vacuum, the presidency has stepped in. So how much do you think that filibuster has played a role in this?

* * *

Martha Joynt Kumar: It's become such a polarized system. People are unwilling to negotiate with one another in key ways that they did in the past. Look at the way that people like Ted Cruz try to stop political appointees. The cabinet secretary got through all right, but you've had the vice president come in and vote on over a dozen appointees. It's become such a polarized system that people are unwilling to negotiate. We no longer have people like John Bailey, chair of the DNC [Democratic National Convention] under Kennedy. He did a lot of work building party loyalty. And we no longer have that kind of work within a party. And the loyalty to a party—it's a loyalty to who your funders are and the constituents that you think are going to actually get to the polls. Those are really factors that drive things like the filibuster, that they get rewarded for politics that step away from the traditional compromise and negotiation. That's why we all thought Biden would, with all of his experiences, legislative experience, would have success. But the people who inhabit the Senate now are not the people who were there when he was there.

* * *

Tevi Troy: Is there anything to be done? Is there a policy prescription that either of you would advocate for how the presidency has changed in the twenty-first century?

* * *

Jonathan Burks: I do think it's become unbalanced. I don't think it's as dire necessarily as some critics, but I do think that it's become unbalanced. The first step is for Congress to take back its authorities in terms of appropriations—in particular, getting back to regularly appropriating funds for the operations of the executive branch. Doing it every time gives Congress a powerful tool to hold the executive to account and to manage and enforce the executive to engage it as a policy equal. It won't solve everything, but it's a good first step.

* * *

Elaine Kamarck: What I would do is a reorientation of the White House staff. And . . . you need a strong communications team, but you need a strengthening of what used to be called "cabinet affairs." These days, cabinet affairs is, "What's the president's message this week? Let's send the cabinet secretaries out to talk about this, that, or the other thing." It's a waste of time, frankly. Nobody really cares if the secretary of agriculture is talking about the Build Back Better bill. But they keep doing it, even though it doesn't ever seem to work. It starts with how he puts together the cabinet. He's got to put together a cabinet with executive experience, because only with executive experience can you have people truly prepared for the job. And then he's got to tell the cabinet, "Go look at that agency and tell me what's good and what's bad. What's going right? And what's going to blow up in my face and ruin the rest of my beautiful policy agenda?" White Houses are about communications and policy, and they are not about operations. And yet it is operations that kills them in the end. And so, I would reorient the White House staff and the cabinet towards an emphasis on operations, both to avoid messes and disasters and also to know when something comes at you out of the blue, as it always does. Know what your tools are. Know what's operating well in the government and know how it can be used to deal with the crisis so that you look like a strong and competent leader, as opposed to the four instances that I've been talking about, where the president didn't look strong and didn't look competent and couldn't talk his way out of that problem.

* * *

Tevi Troy: The orientation of the White House staff is really an essential element of how the presidency develops. And one of the premises in all of my books on the presidency has been this notion that the White House staff really comes out of the late Roosevelt administration, the Brownlow Commission, which had this four-word conclusion, "The president needs help." And it really is that that leads to the development of a White House staff as we know today. I do have some insight into this question of cabinet affairs, and it was really in the George H. W. Bush administration that cabinet affairs sort-of became an alternative policymaking mechanism because there was some sclerotic nature to the policy development process and the rest of the White House. Part of it was OMB director Dick Darwin and White House Chief of Staff John Sununu had a tight rein on the controls.

Part of it was [that] a lot of things were coming out of OPD, the Office of Policy Development. Sununu had some very smart, young, talented staffers in Cabinet Affairs in those days, including Jay Lefkowitz and Dan Cass, and they were really trying to generate policy out of cabinet affairs. Now, Josh Bolten was in that White House. He looked at that and he said, "I don't want to see that in the future White House." So, he used that perspective to help shape the George W. Bush White House, in which Jonathan and I both worked, in a way that cabinet affairs did not really have any policymaking role. I think that skepticism of cabinet affairs has continued ever since. So, it's an interesting insight, and there is some history behind it, how it happened: There was a vacuum; cabinet affairs stepped in to fill that vacuum, and then subsequent administrations reigned-in the notion of an expanded cabinet affairs office.

Bush and Clinton
The last president of the twentieth century embraces the first of the twenty-first. President-elect George W. Bush shakes hands with his predecessor, William J. Clinton, in December 2000. Clinton White House photo.

Obama and Biden on Phone
President Barack Obama and his vice president Joe Biden embracing the new technology that would become essential to the twenty-first-century presidency. White House photo by Pete Souza.

Trump on Phone
President Trump in January 2017. The rise of the Internet has shaped and defined the modern presidency so much that access to a smart phone has become an essential part of operating in the highest office. White House photo by Shealah Craighead.

Jen Psaki
"But it is hard in any White House . . . to get outside perspectives and to get more voices in there because there's just the difficulty of surviving the day sometimes." Former Biden administration press secretary Jen Psaki holding a daily briefing in the James Brady room of the White House. White House photo by Cameron Smith.

Cedric Richmond

Former Biden White House director of public engagement Cedric
Richmond (right), alongside President Biden and Louisiana governor
John Bel Edwards, receiving an update regarding Hurricane Ida on Friday,
September 3, 2021. On delivering the president bad news, Richmond's
advice was, "Don't beat around the bush. Don't try to hide the ball,
sugarcoat it, anything like that. Just give it to him straight and he'll absorb
it." White House photo by Cameron Smith.

Mack McLarty

President Bill Clinton's first chief of staff Mack McLarty (right) with Clinton as the president makes a phone call. On the increasingly frenetic pace of the flow of information, McLarty thought, "If you go through that continuum, you'll just see it accelerated. And we thought it was accelerating at lightspeed in the Clinton administration." Clinton White House photo.

Josh Bolten
"Good leaders don't just tolerate criticism, they welcome it." President
George W. Bush's second and final chief of staff, Joshua Bolten, walking
alongside Bush. White House photo by Eric Draper.

Jay Carney
President Obama's former press secretary Jay Carney in the Oval Office with Kathryn Ruemmler, Jennifer Palmieri, Denis McDonough, and Obama on March 7, 2013. His best piece of advice for a future White House official was, "Take advantage of your predecessors of both parties and seek advice from them." White House photo by Pete Souza.

Kellyanne Conway
Kellyanne Conway and President Trump conversing in the White House Colonnade on June 14, 2019. Regarding one-on-one time with the nation's chief executive, Conway said, "Come prepared, have something new and different to say, or to offer or to ask." White House photo from the Office of Counselor Conway.

The Twenty-First-Century Presidency in the External Environment

In addition to making the decisions necessary to manage the large and complex federal government, the president also has the important goal of gaining political support for the president's program. Richard Neustadt famously observed that the power of the presidency is the power to persuade, and the next two essays relate to the president's capacity to persuade. Presidents measure their success on the persuasion front via polls, and pollster Kristen Soltis Anderson shows how policy has changed in the twenty-first century, not just in terms of technology but also with respect to major changes in political alignment. And Kenneth Baer shows how the tools presidents use to persuade have shifted with the advent of new technologies, leading to a revolution in the ways presidents can communicate with the American people.

CHAPTER 4

Presidential Approval Ratings in the Twenty-First Century

Kristen Soltis Anderson

During the 1990s, Hollywood often took dramatic liberties when portraying presidential politics on-screen. *Air Force One* (1997) shows Harrison Ford as the commander in chief fighting off terrorists in hand-to-hand combat aboard his presidential aircraft. Kevin Kline plays an everyman presidential impersonator in 1993's *Dave*, going to the Oval Office as a fill-in in the wake of a presidential medical emergency. In *Independence Day* (1996), actor Bill Pullman plays a president who pilots a fighter jet to fight aliens and prevent the destruction of Earth.

The 1995 romantic comedy *The American President*, directed by *The West Wing* creator Aaron Sorkin, also takes its fair share of liberties, though perhaps not as egregiously. *The American President* follows the challenges faced by President Andrew Shepherd, a widower played by actor Michael Douglas, who is trying to advance his agenda through Congress. President Shepherd meets a fiery environmental lobbyist named Sydney Ellen Wade, played by Annette Benning, and the two begin a relationship. When Wade's past as a progressive activist is unearthed, it causes public relations headaches for the White House. President Shepherd's job approval begins to collapse.

The president's pollster Leon Kodak is summoned to brief the White House team on the president's political situation. Kodak explains that the president's job approval has fallen precipitously in the wake of his relationship, describing the country as having "mood swings." Chief adviser Lewis Rothschild, played by Michael J. Fox, is exasperated by this explanation: "Mood swings? Nineteen post-graduate degrees in mathematics and your best explanation for going from a 63 to a 46 percent approval rating in five weeks is mood swings?"[1] With job approval numbers that plunge even further as the film goes on, President Shepherd finds even members of his own party less and less willing to support his agenda.

What *The American President* gets right about public opinion and politics is twofold. First is the reliance on public opinion data as an indicator of the national mood and a driver of strategy in a White House. The rise of public opinion polling as a valued input is a major and evolving feature of American presidencies since at least the presidency of Franklin D. Roosevelt. Political scientists James Druckman and Lawrence Jacobs, in reviewing presidential archives, have found that the amount of polling consumed by American presidential administrations increased precipitously from the Kennedy to Reagan administrations, rising from just over a dozen polls conducted by pollster Louis Harris for President John F. Kennedy to over two hundred polls for President Ronald Reagan conducted by pollsters such as Robert Teeter and Richard Wirthlin.[2] By the 1990s, pollsters such as Stan Greenberg—hopefully an inspiration for the character of Leon Kodak—were regularly providing updates to President Bill Clinton and his team on his standing with the American people.[3]

The other thing *The American President* gets correct is the relationship between job approval and a president's ability to implement his or her agenda, bringing Congress along. As political scientists John Lovett, Shaun Bevan, and Frank Baumgartner put it, "Popular presidents can direct congressional attention, at least for a little while . . . unpopular presidents, by contrast, are irrelevant."[4] While a president in his or her first term obviously seeks strong approval ratings in hopes of being reelected, even presidents who are not seeking reelection require public support to maintain agenda-setting influence. Just as President Shepherd struggled to advance his crime bill with a job approval that had fallen near just 40 percent, presidents can reasonably expect the fortunes of their agenda to be tied to their standing with the public.

But though the film gets those two critical components right, a president's job approval swinging by nearly twenty points in a matter of mere weeks feels very disconnected from our current political reality. The United States today looks quite different than it did at the end of the twentieth century and the Clinton administration. The Internet has gone from being emerging technology to being fully embedded in our way of life. News consumption has become ever more fragmented, and cable news has nationalized large pieces of our political debate. Rapid technological, social, and economic changes have left many feeling disoriented, exacerbating the divide between the beneficiaries of those changes and everyone else.

Against that backdrop, we find presidential job approval these days remaining "low and steady"—rarely creeping too far above 50 percent and tending to trade within a narrow band. Americans give institutions of all sorts lower and lower ratings relative to decades ago, and the presidency is no exception. Additionally, yesterday's twenty-point swing in job approval is today's five-point swing. Our increasing political polarization has only further stabilized presidential job approval by creating a high floor and a low ceiling for administrations, with fellow partisans overwhelmingly likely to say they support the incumbent come hell or high water and opposing partisans unlikely to give any credit to a sitting president no matter what.

Presidential job approval has long been viewed as one of the most critical, fundamental metrics for understanding American politics. In the same way that indicators such as the unemployment rate or stock market give us valuable information about the economic environment, presidential job approval is one of the core indicators of the mood of the nation. Even on issues where the evidence suggests presidents have limited influence, such as the economy, presidents are held sometimes singularly responsible by the public for the state of things in the country.[5]

Additionally, presidential job approval has the benefit of being a metric that has been tracked consistently since the advent of modern public opinion polling. While some questions such as issue handling or specific probes on hot-button issues of the moment may not have been standard practice decades ago, polling powerhouses like Gallup have been tracking presidential job approval in a consistent fashion since the days of President Harry Truman. This gives researchers more of an ability to do apples-to-apples comparisons over history and between administrations.

What the long view shows is striking. First, job approval today seems to be lower in general than in past decades. Looking exclusively at data from Gallup, from presidents Truman through Richard Nixon, their first term was characterized by job approvals of well over 50 percent. Numbers that a president today could only dream of were standard during the presidencies of Dwight D. Eisenhower and Kennedy. This has ebbed and flowed over time, of course; while Presidents Gerald Ford and Jimmy Carter each had a lackluster, average job approval during their time in office (averaging 47.2 percent and 45.5 percent, respectively), average approval rebounded slightly for Reagan's first term (averaging 50.3 percent) and George H. W. Bush's term in office (average approval 60.9 percent). But since the turn of the millennium, with the exception of George W. Bush's unprecedented skyrocketing job approval in the immediate aftermath of 9/11, no other president since then has averaged a first-term job approval over 50 percent.

Some of this is just a reflection of poorer attitudes toward leaders and institutions in general. From the 1970s through much of the 2000s, between one-third and one-half of Americans tended to say they approved of the job Congress was doing, a figure that these days sits closer to one-quarter.[6] Institutions like the US Supreme Court have not been tracked for as long but also are seeing record-low job approval figures.[7] Trust in institutions like the media goes lower and lower with each passing year.[8] In short, Americans are less satisfied with most parts of our political life these days, and the presidency is among the most prominent examples.

But some of this is also a factor of a reduced benefit of the doubt from those of the other party. This manifests in a few ways, the first of which is the shrinking of the presidential "honeymoon" period. As Gallup analyst Jeffrey Jones wrote, "Presidents typically receive relatively high job approval ratings when they take office . . . [yet] presidents since 1980 have not had quite as lofty early-term ratings as their predecessors."[9] Prior to 1980, even presidents who wound up with relatively low average job approvals, such as Ford and Carter, began their presidencies with job approvals well north of 60 percent. From Reagan through Obama, presidents still retained a mild "honeymoon" but with job approvals closer to 60 percent.

Meanwhile, neither Donald Trump nor Joe Biden began their presidencies with job approvals very close to 60 percent. In the lead-up to the 2020 election, Pew Research Center found that nine out of ten partisans felt that if the opposing party's candidate won the presidency, it would cause "lasting harm" to the country—hardly an environment conducive to any sort of honeymoon opportunity.[10] Any window of opportunity for a president to push through key pieces of their agenda with the political wind in their sails has gotten narrower and narrower, even in situations where the president's own party has substantial control in the legislative branch.

The demise of the "honeymoon" is likely related to out-party voters simply being more polarized and as a result being less likely to say they approve of the president. From Eisenhower onward, most presidents start out with job approvals well north of 75 percent from their own partisans. What has changed most markedly in recent decades are shifts in how voters of the opposition party view the president. While Trump and Biden got barely any "honeymoon" whatsoever, even the initially popular President Obama had a honeymoon that was relatively limited. After reviewing a wide range of polls tracking presidential job approval, Marquette University professor Charles Franklin found that to the extent Obama had a honeymoon at all, it was due to the fact that he briefly had approval from just over one-third of Republicans—support that all but evaporated by the end of his first year in office.[11]

Pew analyzed presidential job approval ratings going back to Eisenhower, examining their own data as well as that of Gallup, and their findings are striking. They break presidential job approval out by party and find that prior to the Clinton era, presidents tended to garner the approval of at least one-third of those in the opposition party—and often *much* more early in the presidency. Nearly half of all Democrats on average said they approved of the job Eisenhower did as president, and a similar dynamic prevailed with Kennedy. While Nixon, Carter, and Ford all fared less well with the opposition party, they still generally had two to three times as much approval from the out-party's voters as did Obama, Trump, or these days President Biden.[12]

If a president is less and less able to garner the approval of much of *anyone* from the opposition party, the ceiling for a president's job approval becomes lower and lower. Even if a president runs up the score among their own voters, their overall numbers will never be able to achieve the heights of previous decades so long as they are only able to scrape by in the single digits with opposing partisans.

Political scientists have engaged in considerable debate over many decades about just how stable partisanship is as a variable. While a person's partisan identification is not set in stone, it is generally considered more stable at an individual level than one's attitudes about a variety of other things.[13] Someone might change their mind about whether they like a person or how they feel about the world around them, but they are typically much slower to shake off a partisan label with which they have identified. However, as partisanship becomes a stronger predictor of how someone feels about the incumbent president, a variable like presidential job approval will begin to exhibit some of that same characteristic stability.

When running for president, Donald Trump famously said, "I could stand in the middle of Fifth Avenue and shoot somebody, and I wouldn't lose any voters, OK?"[14] As crude as that statement may have been, as a matter of political analysis, it would not wind up being so far off the mark. Despite the turbulence of the Trump presidency, his support among Republicans barely took a hit at any point, underscoring the extent to which partisanship and approval of the president had become deeply intertwined.

In Pew's analysis, no president since Eisenhower had averaged a *higher* job approval from their own party than President Trump (averaging 87 percent approval among Republicans). At the same time, Trump's average job approval among all voters—only 41.1 percent in Gallup polling—ranks at the very bottom of modern presidents' first terms, trailing even Jimmy Carter's weak 45.5 percent average approval.

At only one year in, data suggested a similar dynamic emerged for President Biden's job approval. Among self-identified Democrats, Biden began with job approval of 92 percent, a figure that had fallen only slightly by July to 83 percent. Meanwhile, his "honeymoon" job approval of 13 percent among self-identified Republicans barely budged, sitting at a mere 6 percent in July.[15]

All of this leads to a relatively lackluster job approval being the new normal for presidents. Having sky-high support from one's own party and nearly nonexistent support from the out-party means the range of possible job approval numbers is much narrower and is largely dependent upon big swings in the views of the remaining political independents.

Real Clear Politics' average of all presidential job approval polls showed Trump hitting a first-year high of 46 percent job approval and a first-year low of 37 percent job approval—a nine-point range. In contrast, Biden's first-year high was 56 percent but fell to a first-year low of 41 percent, a wider fifteen-point range. While Biden's job approval has experienced a slightly wider "trading range" than Trump's did in the first year in office, the difference has been entirely attributable to the massive drop-off in approval among self-identified independents, falling in Gallup polling from sixty-one points upon inauguration to 34 percent by October.[16]

If presidents can no longer count on getting more than negligible support from those of the opposing party no matter what they do, maintaining their own base of supporters along with whatever margins they can muster from the remaining independents becomes ever more critical. Efforts to persuade those of the other party are set by the wayside. Administrations will likely become less and less interested in getting their message in front of voters of the other side, considering such effort to generally be wasted. (Biden administration press secretary Jen Psaki has noted that one of the few reasons why administration officials would ever appear on a network like Fox News is that disseminating information about public health remains a priority when it comes to all audiences.)[17]

To the extent that there are efforts at "bipartisanship" at all, they are likely to send a signal to the group of independents in the middle rather than constitute a genuine effort to persuade voters of the other party. While voters often tell pollsters that they value bipartisanship, in practice it is not always rewarded. Consider that neither President Trump's efforts at bipartisan criminal justice reform nor President Biden's efforts at bipartisan infrastructure reform seem to have won over any *voters* from the other side, even as they did create cross-partisan coalitions of political elites to achieve policy ends. The opportunity to win over partisans of the other party seems so minimal that any president looking to build a majority coalition is far likelier to shore up their own partisans, first and foremost.

All of this is occurring in a time when the legislative branch has ceded more and more power to the executive, empowering a president to act even in the absence of a majority coalition in the legislature. From President Obama's "pen and phone" approach in 2014 to the large number of executive actions taken during subsequent administrations, presidents have begun calculating that temporary executive action may well be more beneficial than the hard work of trying to cultivate a legislative win.[18]

The effect of this deep polarization is to make it harder for presidents to achieve anything approaching a "mandate" that would force members of the opposing party to compromise or find ways to work together. There are few reasons for other elected leaders to feel pressure to work with a president of the other party these days. Congressional

Democrats did not need to find any common ground with President Trump to win over swing districts and enjoy a "blue wave" in the 2018 midterms, just as congressional Republicans have clearly opted to oppose President Biden's agenda and nevertheless were well-poised heading into the 2022 midterms.

At the extremes, consider the example of former New Jersey governor Chris Christie, accused of "hugging" President Obama during the most nonpartisan of all moments: disaster relief and recovery. After superstorm Sandy caused enormous devastation in the Northeast in the days before the 2012 election, President Obama met with governors of affected states; photos of Christie's handshake greeting of Obama, even given their deeply apolitical circumstance, was nevertheless used against Christie in advertisements during the 2016 Republican presidential primary.[19]

Presidents who have at least *some* popularity with the out-party—or strong popularity with independent voters—may find themselves invited to stand shoulder to shoulder with governors or other leaders who believe they will benefit from the association. Few Republican governors these days are seeking a photo opportunity with President Biden, just as few Democratic governors were eager for a visit from President Trump. The downsides of upsetting one's own team far outweigh the perceived benefit of reaching across the aisle in most cases.

There is plenty of reason to believe that, at least in the near term, presidents will be very limited in their ability to win plaudits from voters of the opposition party. Antipathy toward the other party shows no sign of abating. A working paper by political scientists Matthew Tyler and Shanto Iyengar suggests that our levels of polarization and disdain for those of the other side are "unprecedented," and that this is now even permeating the political views of adolescents who, in previous decades, would have held more positive views of leaders such as the president. Republicans and Democrats continue to get large amounts of news from very different sources and may remain less likely to see positive news coverage about a president of the other party.

In the near term, presidents are just less likely to be widely loved or viewed as unifying figures. On top of the robust polling data reflecting this trend, just look at Hollywood's imagining of the presidency since the turn of the millennium—more likely to make entertainment about fictional presidents who are corrupt and conniving rather than heroic and heartwarming. (Even Hollywood's portrayal of presidential pollsters has become more jaundiced; Gary Cole's portrayal of presidential data wonk Kent Davison on *VEEP* is hilarious but has much sharper edges than the Leon Kodaks of old.)

Distrust and disdain for major institutions permeates culture and yields a world where the presidency is viewed almost exclusively through a partisan lens.

Over the longer term, however, this trend toward generally lower and more constrained job approval is not guaranteed to persist. It was just twenty years ago that a sharply divided nation moved past the wounds of *Bush v. Gore* to rally around President George W. Bush in the wake of the tragedy of September 11. And while the crisis of the COVID-19 pandemic has not had even remotely a similar unifying effect, there is no telling what the future holds. Compelling leadership, a new global crisis, any number of factors—positive and negative—could disrupt the current trend.

NOTES

1. Internet Movie Database, "The American President (1995)," accessed August 10, 2023, https://www.imdb.com/title/tt0112346/characters/nm000 1601.

2. James N. Druckman and Lawrence R. Jacobs, *Who Governs? Presidents, Public Opinion, and Manipulation* (Chicago: University of Chicago Press, 2015).

3. Stanley B. Greenberg, *Dispatches from the War Room: In the Trenches with Five Extraordinary Leaders* (New York: Thomas Dunne, 2009).

4. John Lovett, Shaun Bevan, and Frank R. Baumgardner, "Popular Presidents Can Affect Congressional Attention, for a Little While," *Policy Studies Journal* 43, no. 1 (2015), https://fbaum.unc.edu/articles/PSJ2015Popular Presidents.pdf.

5. Neil Irwin, "Presidents Have Less Power Over the Economy than You Might Think," *New York Times*, January 17, 2017, https://www.nytimes.com /2017/01/17/upshot/presidents-have-less-power-over-the-economy-than -you-might-think.html.

6. "Congress and the Public," Gallup, accessed January 6, 2022, https:// news.gallup.com/poll/1600/congress-public.aspx.

7. "Supreme Court," Gallup, accessed January 6, 2022, https://news.gal lup.com/poll/4732/supreme-court.aspx.

8. Megan Brenan, "Americans' Trust in Media Dips to Second Lowest on Record," Gallup, October 7, 2021, https://news.gallup.com/poll/355526 /americans-trust-media-dips-second-lowest-record.aspx.

9. Jeffrey M. Jones, "Trump Approval More Stable than Approval for Prior Presidents," Gallup, December 21, 2018, https://news.gallup.com/opinion /polling-matters/245567/trump-approval-stable-approval-prior-presidents.aspx.

10. Michael Dimock and Richard Wike, "America Is Exceptional in Its Political Divide," Pew Trusts, March 29, 2021, https://www.pewtrusts.org/en /trust/archive/winter-2021/america-is-exceptional-in-its-political-divide.

11. Charles Franklin, "Five Things about Trump Approval Polling," Medium, March 7, 2017, https://medium.com/research-at-marquette/five-thing s-about-trump-approval-polling-e86d44f3cbc8#.ptkdtz67k.

12. Amina Dunn, "Trump's Approval Ratings So Far Are Unusually Stable— and Deeply Partisan," Pew Research Center, August 24, 2020, https://www.pew research.org/fact-tank/2020/08/24/trumps-approval-ratings-so-far-are-unu sually-stable-and-deeply-partisan/.

13. Donald Philip Green and Bradley Palmquist, "How Stable Is Party Identification?" *Political Behavior* 16, no. 4 (1994): 437–66, http://www.jstor.org /stable/586469.

14. Colin Dwyer, "Donald Trump: 'I Could . . . Shoot Somebody, and I Wouldn't Lose Any Voters,'" NPR, January 23, 2016, https://www.npr.org /sections/thetwo-way/2016/01/23/464129029/donald-trump-i-could-shoot -somebody-and-i-wouldnt-lose-any-voters.

15. "Biden Loses Ground with the Public on Issues, Personal Traits and Job Approval," Pew Research Center, September 2021, https://www.pewresearch .org/politics/2021/09/23/biden-loses-ground-with-the-public-on-issues-per sonal-traits-and-job-approval/.

16. Jeffrey Jones, "Biden Job Approval Steady at Lower Level," Gallup, October 22, 2021, https://news.gallup.com/poll/356504/biden-job-approval -steady-lower-level.aspx.

17. Martin Pengelly, "Psaki: We Engage with Fox News in Hope Viewers Might Listen to Medical Experts," *Guardian*, July 26, 2021, https://www.the guardian.com/us-news/2021/jul/26/jen-psaki-fox-news-peter-doocy-covid -vaccinations-hannity-tucker-carlson.

18. Tamara Keith, "Wielding a Pen and a Phone, Obama Goes It Alone," NPR, January 20, 2014, https://www.npr.org/2014/01/20/263766043/wield ing-a-pen-and-a-phone-obama-goes-it-alone.

19. Zeke Miller, "Christie: Obama 'Hug' Never Happened," *Time*, February 4, 2016, https://time.com/4207368/chris-christie-barack-obama-hug/.

CHAPTER 5

Communications and the Presidency in the Twenty-First Century

Kenneth S. Baer

When I first joined the office of the vice president's communications team in the late summer of 1999, I was issued a pager so whoever needed me could "beep" me to get to the nearest telephone and call the office. Ten years later, upon joining the Obama administration, I was handed a Blackberry smartphone, which buzzed whenever I was emailed or called, prompting an immediate, thumb-driven response. And as I left that position at the end of the first term, White House appointees were starting to use Apple iPhones and scrambling for Twitter handles to stay plugged-in to the day's ever-evolving news.

These leaps in technological capabilities changed how White House staffers communicated with each other and illustrates how the White House changed how it communicated with the public. It is cliche to say that the Internet has transformed every aspect of our lives over the past two decades, but that does not mean that this is not true. The presidency is no exception. Near-ubiquitous, high-speed Internet and smartphone usage, plus the rise of social media networks run on both, have transformed how the White House relates to the media and public at large, with profound implications for democracy and governance.

This chapter will put a particular focus on the Obama administration—not just because of my firsthand experience in it, but also because the eight years of the Obama presidency straddle two significant eras in the rise of digital media. The first is a "prealgorithmic" era in which there is a proliferation of digital media outlets, but social media use is still limited. The second is an "algorithmic" era in which social media platforms—Facebook, YouTube, and especially Twitter—begin to predominate, shaping media coverage as well as the actions of the presidency itself.

THE RISE OF TV

Deep into the twentieth century, presidents rarely employed—in the words of political scientist Samuel Kernell—a "going public" strategy to rally public support for their policy agenda in Washington, DC. Instead, they relied on bargaining and log-rolling with Congress, far from the media spotlight.[1] That is why the amount of political travel to drive local news coverage, press conferences, and speeches in Washington and around the country—which now seem part and parcel of the modern presidency—were rare in the 1950s and 1960s. Indeed, presidents in those two decades averaged 151 speeches a year compared to four hundred a year during the 1980s and 1990s.[2]

Presidents started to appeal to the public to move their agenda for a variety of reasons. To start, it was easier: satellite feeds made it possible to transmit footage live across the country. Also, it suited who the president was. Ronald Reagan—the former actor known as the "Great Communicator"—and his team were keenly aware of the importance of television and staging for it to drive their message; how they did both changed the modern presidency. Underneath this were larger trends reshaping US politics such as weaker parties and politicians more reliant on raising their own money and running their own campaigns. In such a world, rallying public support for one's agenda, especially in the relevant district or state, would have more currency with a member of Congress than, for instance, appeals to party loyalty and, in many cases, would be essential to win the support of a member of Congress.

While it was founded a decade earlier, by 1990, CNN—the cable news channel—and the start of the Gulf War increased in prominence, further accelerating the aforementioned dynamics, creating a twenty-four-hour news cycle and a large demand for news content. From one side, this meant that a president's—or presidential candidate's—utterances on the trail in a remote corner of New Hampshire could become national news instantly. From the other side, it created more opportunities to craft moments to be covered—whether those were lunchtime remarks, a visit to a local school, or comments on the way to *Marine One*, the presidential helicopter. With CNN on air, there was no "return to normal programming" until the evening newscast; covering, commenting on, and arguing about the news was the normal programming.

As the twenty-first century began, the news media were everywhere and on all the time. Video could be captured and transmitted from every corner of the country at any time of day. Print reporters could file a story any place there was a regular phone line, and the publications they worked for had the resources to hire the reporters needed to cover a president and those aspiring to the office. Presidents relied on the media to communicate with the American people in order to push their agenda in Washington, and the breadth and depth of those outlets provided them with many avenues to do so.

In many ways, this status quo persisted into the George W. Bush presidency. The president used national addresses and stagecrafted moments to communicate his message. Accordingly, the Bush administration booked presidential travel to promote its legislative agenda to local media outlets and the now proliferation of cable channels. Recall that on September 11, 2001, Bush was reading a children's book to second graders in a Sarasota, Florida, classroom to promote his education agenda, a normal activity for a president on what became an abnormal day. To the extent that people were going online, it was to read news articles that they would not necessarily see otherwise via the site of another city's newspaper or through aggregators of links such as the Drudge Report or AL Daily.

There were signs of change, however. The one innovation in digital media during the Bush presidency was the appearance and influence of the "blogosphere," a shorthand term for the weblogs (aka blogs) that featured the opinions, instant reactions, and, in some cases, reporting of individual voices. This included reported opinion sites such as the center-left Talking Points Memo, former *New Republic* editor Andrew Sullivan's the Daily Dish, Glenn Reynolds's Instapundit, Taegan Goddard's Political Wire, and the Daily Kos, which became a force on the Left. Bloggers could bring to light stories that the mainstream media missed (such as comments that the then Senate Majority Leader Trent Lott made about Strom Thurmond's Dixiecrat run for president, which ultimately led to Lott's resignation), offer expert insights that the blogger's uniquely had, or serve up instant "takes" on the news as it happened. As part of this, "live-blogging" became a way in real time for an audience to follow an event and for an author to spin what was happening. In many ways, blogs were just like any other media outlet and could be treated as such, yet, with their low barrier of entry and ways that they could influence mainstream media, they also foreshadowed how communication would change.

THE OBAMA PRESIDENCY

Four months after Senator Barack Obama announced his presidential candidacy, the Apple iPhone went on sale in the United States. Both portended massive changes in how new media would be used on the campaign trail and in the White House. Indeed, the 2008 Obama campaign was the first presidential campaign to use the Internet and Web 2.0 strategically; that is, not just use the web as a place to post campaign information on a relatively static website. They used their own website, growing social networks such as Facebook and Myspace, video sites such as the then-three-year-old YouTube, and text messages and emails to organize millions of supporters and raise millions of dollars. For instance, two million supporters created profiles at MyBarackObama. com and organized more than thirty-five thousand supporter groups and one hundred and fifty thousand events through the site. Obama garnered 3.1 million Facebook friends, 987,923 Myspace friends, and three million online donors. The campaign created nearly two thousand official YouTube videos that were viewed more than eighty million times. Across all these scores, the Obama campaign lapped that of John McCain, the Republican opponent: McCain had one-quarter the YouTube viewers, one-fifth the number of Facebook friends, and half the website traffic of Obama.[3] While the media coverage of Obama was extensive (and to some critics fawning), digital media and platforms on which to share this content became a way for the Obama campaign to "go around" the traditional media and communicate with and organize its supporters.

When the Obama team entered the White House, it inherited a digital media infrastructure from an earlier era. The White House website was a collection of important documents, such as press releases and speech transcripts, issued by the Executive Office of the President. For cybersecurity reasons, special permission was required to visit social media sites such as Facebook and Twitter (the latter growing in prominence), and further clearance was necessary to create an account on either site for official matters.

Not wanting to abandon what it accomplished on the campaign trail, the Obama team established the Office of New Media, which included the first presidential videographer to document the president as much as the official photographer does, as well as graphic designers and content and engagement specialists. As the office's name connotes, this operation ran alongside the traditional media and communications operations of the White House, and its focus was to use the production and dissemination capabilities and advantages of new media to put content out directly to the public and unfiltered through the press. That is, its primary focus was not to shape or "spin" the media but to "go around" it—effectively, to be its own media outlet. This included photos of the day and videos about happenings and accomplishments of the White House, fact sheets, and blog posts. It also included novel ways to explain policies directly to the public. Take the "White House White Board" series. It debuted on September 30, 2010, with Council of Economic Advisers (CEA) chair Austan Goolsbee taking to a whiteboard to explain the administration's position on tax policy and attack the position of congressional Republicans.[4] This format was later used to explain difficult policy topics such as Obama's proposal on mortgage refinance and the American Taxpayer Relief Act of 2012, and it was even resurrected recently in the Biden White House.[5]

Or consider the use of blogs by the Obama White House. In the pre-Internet age, the White House press release was the only way to deliver news (and it was done via the news media who could choose to cover it or not). Now, the White House—like anyone—had no barriers to creating content. This meant that, over time, blogs were used by a myriad of White House offices to put out their own targeted messages (this author's grandmother's recipe for apple kugel was shared during Passover on a White House blog as part of outreach to the Jewish American community).[6]

For example, the Office of Management and Budget (OMB) was the first component of the Executive Office of the President to create its own blog, *OMBlog*. Motivated by what OMB director Peter Orszag saw as the advantages having a blog afforded him when he ran the Congressional Budget Office and the experience his associate director in charge of communications had as a writer in the blogosphere, they used *OMBlog* to highlight aspects of the agency's work that may be overlooked (such as procurement reform or evidence-based policy-making), explain complicated budgetary or economic concepts, roll out more obscure policy initiatives, and rebut critics.[7] During the fight to pass the Affordable Care Act, for instance, *OMBlog* was particularly useful as the debates became more complex, heated, and constant.[8] A blogpost was an effective way to inject one's views into the quickening news cycle. Using *OMBlog* in these ways enabled the agency leadership to put out "news" without any external editorial judgment, without risking being thrown off track by a hard question in a live media briefing, and with the administration's rationales unchallenged. If and when the media inquired about a specific topic, the OMB communications office could easily direct the reporter to the blog explaining it all.

The Obama team saw these new digital media not only as a way to go around the traditional media but also as a tool for citizen engagement, an important goal of Obama and an important part of his presidential campaign. The Office of New Media, for instance, started Internet town hall meetings in which anyone could submit a question online to be answered. At first, one hundred thousand questions were sent in and were ranked in importance by 3.5 million people.[9] Tens of thousands of people voted for winners of OMB's SAVE Award, an award given to the federal employee with the best idea to cut wasteful spending, and the White House launched "We the People" petitions in which any petition that received at least one hundred thousand "signatures" online would receive a response from a high-level official. From its founding in September 2011 to its closure in December 2016, We the People gathered approximately four hundred and eighty thousand petitions, twenty-nine million users, and forty million signatures.[10]

While the White House moved to embrace these new ways to engage the public directly, it still had to contend with the press corps itself, which was wrestling with the new digital media landscape. From 2006 to 2008, daily online new use increased by one-third, with one-quarter of all Americans getting their news online.[11] In response to plunging ad revenue, traditional media outlets, such as the major regional newspapers (such as the *Hartford Courant, San Jose Mercury News,* and others), drastically curtailed their coverage of Washington and of the presidency with some closing bureaus altogether and many forgoing covering the president as he traveled (news organizations need to pay the White House for travel). Cable news—which now included MSNBC and Fox News—became increasingly partisan and had an insatiable demand for stories to cover. As a result, senior White House aides and policy officials who proved their ability to joust on air with cable TV hosts would supplement the White House press secretary's daily briefing with three-minute interviews on "Pebble Beach," the filming area on the front lawn of the White House. At the same time, the digital press matured beyond the blogosphere to news sites such as Talking Points Memo, the Daily Beast, and Huffington Post, which combined traditional reporting with opinion pieces, a partisan point of view, and, in some cases, videos and "listicles" to garner more clicks. Reflecting this new reality, President Obama made history in his first presidential news conference in March 2009 when he became the first president to call on a reporter from a digital-only publication, Sam Stein of the Huffington Post.[12]

Altogether this created a news cycle that never ended. "As media outlets multiply and it becomes easier to disseminate information on the Web and on cable," wrote longtime media critic Ken Auletta in 2010: "The news cycle is getting shorter—to the point that there is no pause, only the constancy of the Web and the endless argument of cable."[13] For reporters, this meant that instead of filing a handful—or fewer—stories a week and having hours to report even breaking news, they were creating content all day with a deadline of now: quick online articles, TV appearances to comment on the news, podcasts, blogs, tweets, and Facebook posts. For the press staff that needed to interact with them, every day was like drinking from the proverbial fire hose with a seemingly endless stream of questions that needed to be answered correctly in terms of facts and message. It also had to be answered quickly as the reporter, under huge pressure to be first, would just post the story writing that "the Administration was unavailable for comment." If that happened, this would invite questions from communications officials in the West Wing as to why the spokesperson was not getting the president's message out there. Especially in the eventful first two years of the Obama administration, a press spokesman could wake at 5 a.m. and spend the next eighteen hours doing nothing else but fielding questions from the media.

This never-ending news cycle not only created a huge demand for content but also a fierce competition for readers or "eyeballs" (the metric of choice in digital media). This rewarded conflict and controversy and disadvantaged coverage of the far-less dramatic introduction of a policy initiative or a new regulation. Similarly, politicians, advocates, or commentators willing to use heated language, indulge in wild allegations and speculation, and to "call out" the administration or one of its officials made great TV guests, bloggers, and social media stars. That, combined with the lack of editorial judgment that came with the democratization of content creation, gave prominence to those willing to indulge in that behavior and, at its worst, gave oxygen to wild conspiracy theories and accusations that could be lodged in a corner of the Internet and make their way into the mainstream media. One needs only to follow the life cycle of the claims that President Obama was not born in America and that the Affordable Care Act included "death panels" to understand how this worked.

Supercharging all of these trends toward the end of Obama's first term and into his second was the rise of Twitter. The microblogging, social media site was still a novelty in the first years of the Obama presidency. During the 2008 campaign, for instance, the Obama team had a Twitter account and posted 262 tweets from April 29, 2007, until December 5, 2008, and upwards of 80 percent of the tweets were used to inform followers of where Obama was on any given day.[14] In the White House, Twitter usage started similarly. Yet, over time, it became clear that as more and more reporters and thought-leaders joined the service, it became a crucial way to understand what they were thinking or working on. Because of this, more communications staffers—and some principals—wanted a Twitter account.

But not everyone was convinced that this was wise or appropriate. In July 2011, for example, the then OMB director Jack Lew was presented with a memo outlining why the agency, and possibly he, should have a Twitter account. The memo noted that not only were many other Cabinet-level agencies and White House officials joining the service but even the Pope was tweeting. Reflecting the norms of a fading era, Lew felt that it would definitely be improper for the OMB director or the agency itself to be engaging on such a platform. Yet even Lew recognized that the world was changing and that to effectively communicate at least the communications function of the agency it needed to be on Twitter. On July 19, 2011, @OMBPress was launched.

Being on Twitter accelerated the news cycle even more—bringing to light controversies and stories in real time. Soon, the OMB communications office was monitoring it constantly and used the platform as a way to inject news into the conversation—for instance, using Twitter to alert the media about "Statements of Administration Policy" (SAP), the official stance taken by the White House on a piece of pending legislation and how veto threats were issued.

While the start of the OMB Twitter account will not warrant a footnote in even an exhaustive history of the Obama administration, it is emblematic of how fast the media environment was changing as the first Obama term ended. Indeed, a new phase in digital media was emerging—an algorithmic era in which data-driven, social media platforms that monetized users' attention dominated. These platforms—such as Twitter, YouTube, and Facebook—took information gleaned from a user's interaction from the site and, even across the Internet, tailored content to his or her preferences. The content selected were those that were the most popular or "viral," putting a greater premium on not just the cute and frivolous but also the controversial, combative, and bombastic. Moreover, the algorithms would learn a user's interests and opinions, thus reinforcing their own biases. These echo chambers made it much easier to spread lies and untruths and untethered millions of Americans from traditional media for information about the president. As longtime Obama communications aide Dan Pfeiffer explained, "After the 2012 election . . . the penetration of the traditional press was becoming significantly diminished. We were having trouble getting the message we wanted to get out, but at the same time, because of the power of social media, the messages that other people wanted to get out about us were breaking through to people."[15]

In Obama's second term, Twitter was increasingly shaping coverage and the conversation in the Beltway. The communications office could not just go around the media; rather, it had to go through the new media platforms to find specific audiences. This meant creating content that could go viral on Twitter and Facebook, from GIFs and videos to even lighting up the White House itself in rainbow colors when the Supreme Court upheld gay marriage (an image made for social media that ricocheted across Twitter, Instagram, and Facebook). The communications staff sent Obama on a variety of new media outlets such as Jerry Seinfeld's *Comedians in Cars Getting Coffee* show on Netflix, booked him on podcasts such as Marc Maron's *WTF* (recorded in the comedian's garage), and placed him on YouTube shows such as the comedian Zach Galifianakis's *Between Two Ferns* and GloZell Green's show in order to reach her three million followers.[16] This was not just a long way from *Meet the Press* but also a long way from twenty years earlier when a presidential candidate playing the saxophone in sunglasses on a late-night TV talk show was considered shocking.

TRUMP AND TWITTER

While the Obama team was pushing the envelope by placing the president in nontraditional outlets, there was a limit to how far they would go to get attention. That is, neither the president nor his team would create conflict unnecessarily even though it would yield more clicks. A fidelity to facts, whether driven by ethics or a fear of being fact-checked by the traditional media, meant that any content produced by the White House was reviewed just as closely by the research department as a congressional address (this author recalls the fact-checking of his children's names for the caption of a White House "photo of the day"). And even though the traditional media was diminished in importance and often seemed to be trapped chasing online controversies and rumors that infuriated the White House communications team, administration spokespeople saw themselves as public servants who owed the media a truthful response. There was a widespread and deeply held sentiment that any deviation from the truth could cause a scandal that would hurt your boss, most likely lead to your firing, and blow up your career.

Obama's successor, Donald Trump, and his administration saw things differently. They disregarded these norms and embraced the new algorithmic era wholeheartedly. Trump came to the presidency not only with unique communication abilities as a many yearslong TV performer but also with a keen appreciation of the growing role of social media platforms gained through his own use of Twitter. He and his team had no compunction with creating conflict and controversy; indeed, they used social media to attack the media who then increased their coverage of the attack and the administration! In more than 26,000 tweets, Trump used the service to shape the coverage of his presidency day in and day out.[17] He taunted his political opponents with puerile nicknames, made wild claims, and amplified the views of marginal, if not extreme, voices online. All of this was tailor-made to go viral on Twitter and, in turn, to affect the media coverage.

At the same time, one of the real risks of the White House's ability to create its own content and communicate it directly to the public was that it could cross the line into regime propaganda with a tenuous hold on reality. At the very first briefing by the White House press secretary, it was clear that this line was going to be crossed as attendance numbers to the Trump inauguration were made up. Facts were not going to get in the way of what the Trump White House said, wrote, or released to the media. It is beyond the scope of this paper to detail all the examples of lies, untruths, and misinformation generated by the Trump administration. Suffice it to say that according to the *Washington Post*'s fact-checking team, Trump himself uttered 30,573 "untruths" over his presidency, averaging twenty-one lies a day.[18]

All in all, Trump had little regard for the media, seeing them at best as an institution to be bypassed and at worst as an enemy of the people. It is no surprise that he was the first president in the modern era to have a White House press secretary who did not once brief the press on camera and went the longest—more than a year—without an on-camera White House press briefing since those had started in the Clinton era.[19] While Trump may have professed his disdain for the mainstream media, he understood it in its present form better than any other politician. Trump saw how Twitter complemented, and served as a catalyst to, the twenty-four–hour news cycle and that Twitter had a unique hold on the news media and political elites who influenced it and read it. He then used Twitter to shape and guide press coverage of his presidency. This was a far cry from the promise of digital media at the start of the era; namely, that it would be a democratizing force, giving a voice to millions, and introducing new perspectives to public debates.

Indeed, Twitter has had a distorting effect on American democracy and governance. It is hard to convey a complex point in a tweet, and there is very little to stop a president from using Twitter or other social media platforms to spread lies or misinformation (it took the January 6 insurrection for Trump to be removed from Twitter).[20] Also, the platform's algorithm highlights accounts that the user likes, rewarding partisanship and the scoring of points on political opponents. More damaging though is that Twitter is deeply unrepresentative of the public at large yet is used as a proxy for popular opinion by those making coverage decisions in newsrooms and policy calls at every level of government.

First, relatively few Americans actually use Twitter. According to a 2021 poll by NBC News, 69 percent of adults reported having a Facebook account compared to 28 percent on Twitter (27 percent don't have an account on Facebook, Twitter, or TikTok).[21] An earlier Pew poll from 2019 also found that the most active 10 percent of users are responsible for 80 percent of all tweets created by US users.[22]

Second, Twitter users lean markedly to the left of the political spectrum. The NBC News poll found that while 38 percent of all adults polled reported positive feelings toward former President Trump, only 19 percent of Twitter users did. Similarly, when asked which party they preferred to control Congress, 47 percent of all voters and 65 percent of Twitter users said Democrats. Pew found similar results: 43 percent of US adults identify as or lean Republican, compared with 35 percent of adult Twitter users. The demographic differences between Twitter users and the general public track with the partisan ones: Twitter users are younger, wealthier, more educated, and whiter than the general population.

Third, not only do Twitter users tilt to the left, but of those who are Democrats, they are further to the left than the rest of the party. According to a 2019 study of Democratic presidential primary voters—historically to the left of all self-identified Democrats—conducted by Third Way, only 12 percent of this group were on Twitter.[23] This minority of Democratic primary voters (and even smaller minority of Democrats) was more concerned with social issues such as abolishing the Immigration and Customs Enforcement agency (64 percent support versus 29 percent of all Democratic primary voters) than with kitchen-table issues such as reducing the cost of health care (24 percent support to 43 percent). Unsurprisingly, these Democrats are twenty-four percentage points more likely than other Democrats to call themselves Democratic Socialists.[24]

While this ideological tilt presents a specific problem for Democrats, it affects elected officials and presidents of all parties because of the agenda-setting and opinion-shaping power that Twitter has among political reporters. Thus, even the Biden administration—which attributed its victory in 2020 to ignoring Twitter—is active on the platform to such a degree that *Politico* notes daily which articles the White House is promoting.

CONCLUSION

The massive upheaval in the media industry over the past two decades, caused by the rise of the Internet, has fundamentally changed how the White House communicates with the American people. No longer are press spokespeople sufficient. A modern White House needs to operate what is, in effect, its own studio—an operation to create video, audio, memes, GIFs, blogs, and other content to put out its message. At the start of this phenomenon, in the Obama first term, this was an effort to go around the media and feed an insatiable twenty-four-hour news cycle. Quickly, though, social media platforms began to proliferate and predominate. In this algorithmic era, there was still a demand for content, but to reach people, it had to go through Twitter, Facebook, YouTube, and the like. This put a premium on showmanship and surprise and, at worst, on conflict and bombast in order to "go viral."

All of this was exploited by candidate and then President Trump who ignored previous norms around presidential rhetoric and fidelity to facts. Even without Trump's election, though, Twitter would have retained its unique popularity among the political news media and political elites. With this comes its own distortions as Twitter users are significantly unrepresentative of America—younger, wealthier, whiter, more educated, and more liberal than the Democratic Party itself and the public at large. This affects what the news media covers, and, more troubling, it affects policymaking as well. As the algorithmic era progresses, we are then left with a situation in which there is more coverage of the comings and goings of the presidency than ever before, but the platforms that are shaping this coverage are distorting the picture the public sees and having a profound impact on policymaking, politics, and the health of the republic.

NOTES

1. Samuel Kernell, *Going Public: New Strategies of Presidential Leadership*, 3rd ed. (Washington, DC: CQ Press, 1997).

2. Matthew Eshbaugh-Soha and Jeffrey S. Peake, *Breaking Through the Noise: Presidential Leadership, Public Opinion, and the News Media* (Stanford, CA: Stanford University Press, 2011), 5.

3. Jennifer Aaker and Victoria Chang, "Obama and the Power of Social Media and Technology," Stanford Graduate School of Business, 2009, https://www.gsb.stanford.edu/faculty-research/case-studies/obama-power-social-media-technology.

4. "White House Whiteboard: CEA Chair Austan Goolsbee Explains the Tax Cut Fight," White House, September 30, 2010, https://obamawhitehouse.archives.gov/photos-and-video/video/2010/09/29/white-house-white-board-cea-chair-austan-goolsbee-explains-tax-cut.

5. White House, "White House Whiteboard: Refinancing," YouTube, April 18, 2012, https://www.youtube.com/watch?v=BhpUiMp6Nlw; and White House, "White House Whiteboard: American Taxpayer Relief Act of 2012," YouTube, January 3, 2013, https://www.youtube.com/watch?v=x_3ty8k1ZgY.

6. Kenneth Baer, "Recipe in Spotlight: Apple Kugel," *White House Blog*, March 28, 2012, https://obamawhitehouse.archives.gov/blog/2012/03/28/recipe-spotlight-apple-kugel.

7. See, for instance, Kenneth Baer, "Taking a Hatchet to the Facts," *White House Blog*, January 28, 2010, https://obamawhitehouse.archives.gov/blog/2010/01/28/taking-a-hatchet-facts.

8. See, for instance: Peter Orszag, "Thinking Long-Term," *White House Blog*, July 8, 2010, https://obamawhitehouse.archives.gov/omb/blog/10/07/08/Thinking-Long-Term.

9. Ken Auletta, "Non-Stop News: With Cable, the Web, and Tweets Can the President—or the Press—Still Control the Story?," *New Yorker*, January 25, 2010, https://www.newyorker.com/magazine/2010/01/25/non-stop-news.

10. "About We the People," White House, accessed January 8, 2022, https://petitions.obamawhitehouse.archives.gov/about/.

11. Auletta, "Non-Stop News."

12. Linda Bergthold, "Obama Calls on Huffington Post's Sam Stein," Huffington Post, March 12, 2009, https://www.huffpost.com/entry/obama-calls-on-huffington_b_165448.

13. Auletta, "Non-Stop News."

14. Frederic I. Solop, "'RT @BarackObama We just made history': Twitter and Social Networks in the 2008 Campaign," in *Communicator-in-Chief: How Barack Obama Used New Media Technology to Win the White House*," ed. John Allen Hendricks and Robert E. Denton Jr. (Lanham, MD: Lexington Books, 2010), 48.

15. Steven Levy, "The Man Who Made Barack Obama Viral," Wired, March 9, 2015, https://www.wired.com/2015/03/the-man-who-made-obama-viral/.

16. See "President Barack Obama: Between Two Ferns with Zach Galifianakis," YouTube, March 13, 2014, https://www.youtube.com/watch?v=UnW3xkHxIEQ.

17. "How Many Tweets?," Trump Twitter Archive, accessed January 8, 2022, https://www.thetrumparchive.com/insights/frequency.

18. Glenn Kessler, Salvador Rizzo, and Meg Kelly, "Trump's False or Misleading Claims Total 30,573 over 4 Years," *Washington Post*, January 24, 2021, https://www.washingtonpost.com/politics/2021/01/24/trumps-false-or-misleading-claims-total-30573-over-four-years/.

19. Kaitlin Collins and Kate Bennett, "Grisham Out as West Wing Press Secretary without Having Held a Briefing," CNN, April 7, 2020, https://www.cnn.com/2020/04/07/politics/stephanie-grisham-press-secretary-briefing-melania-trump/index.html.

20. Kate Conger and Mike Isaac, "Twitter Permanently Bans Trump, Capping Online Revolt," *New York Times*, January 8, 2021, https://www.nytimes.com/2021/01/08/technology/twitter-trump-suspended.html.

21. Chuck Todd, Mark Murray, and Ben Kamisar, "New NBC Poll Shows Deep

Partisan Differences among Social Media Users," NBC News, November 8, 2021, https://www.nbcnews.com/politics/meet-the-press/new-nbc-poll-shows-deep-partisan-differences-among-social-media-n1283453.

22. Stefan Wojcik and Adam Hughes, "Sizing Up Twitter Users," Pew Research Center, April 24, 2019, https://www.pewresearch.org/internet/2019/04/24/sizing-up-twitter-users/.

23. Lanae Erickson and Ryan Pougiales, "Avoiding the Funhouse Mirror Effect in the Democratic Primary," Third Way, June 18, 2019, https://www.thirdway.org/memo/avoiding-the-funhouse-mirror-effect-in-the-democratic-primary.

24. Erickson and Pougiales, "Avoiding the Funhouse Mirror Effect in the Democratic Primary."

The Twenty-First-Century Presidency in the External Environment

Edited version of a conversation at the February 15, 2022, Bipartisan Policy Center conference focusing on how the presidency is viewed in the external environment.

Tevi Troy: Now I'm going to pass it on to Susan Glasser from the *New Yorker*, who wrote a terrific book along with her husband, Peter Baker, *The Man Who Ran Washington*, on James Baker, who I consider to be the greatest chief of staff in White House history.

* * *

Susan Glasser, staff writer, the *New Yorker*: I think it's a really wide range and interesting set of provocations that makes us consider this question of how has the presidency changed over the last few presidencies. I thought we would go ahead and start today with the question, a sort of baseline assumption, about presidents today. And one of the biggest ways in which the presidency has changed the last few years. Kristen Soltis Anderson is a fantastic Republican pollster, and she has really written an important paper that hopefully you can sort of fill us in on that gives us a baseline understanding for that most important question of a modern president going back decades now, which is the question of how does the public view the job they're doing? And there's been a pretty radical shift that she describes in this paper, and it's called "low and steady," which is the new normal when it comes to presidential polling and the approval ratings or disapproval ratings, as the case may be. But Kristen, maybe you can give us just a little bit of a sense of how radical of a shift it is. We're all familiar at this point with the kind of straight-line trend of the Donald Trump presidency, and now to its somewhat lesser extent the Biden presidency. The days when public opinions swung wildly about our president seem to be gone, at least for now. So, help us understand this kind of new normal.

* * *

Kristen Soltis Anderson: Looking at presidential job approval, I term it *low and steady* these days. And it's low and steady for two reasons. First, it's low because people tend to be pretty upset about things these days in a way that they were not as upset consistently in prior decades. We have seen, this is not just about the presidency but trust in all sorts of institutions—the media, other branches of government, what have you; that what used to be a general sense of trust and periodic disapproval has really curdled into Americans feeling that not a lot these days is working, and that bleeds into how they're viewing the presidency as well.

When people just tend to be a bit madder about everything, then that's going to depress your overall numbers. The other factor is that presidents in more modern times have not had as much of a honeymoon. Gallup has thankfully been tracking data on presidential job approval, going back decades and decades and decades. And it used to be the case that when you came into office, there was at least some brief period where you got the benefit of the doubt. You both had a lot of support from your own party, but even large numbers of those in the other party would say, "I don't think they've screwed anything up yet. So, I'll give them the benefit of the doubt." But that honeymoon period really does not exist as much anymore. So, the reason why I think that there's no more honeymoon, again, is linked to the reason why people's job approval is steady. And that's because we have polarization. That's pretty significant. Again, presidents used to be able to get some credit from the other party, and they would also get some criticism from their own. But nowadays people are really unlikely to say that they like much of what the other party's president is doing. With Biden as the example, CNN released a poll last week that asked people, "Well, even if you disapprove of the job Biden is doing, is there anything he's doing that you like?" And the statistically significant number of people in that question said, "Well, he got a cat." So, it's very hard to get people to say that they will give credit to the other party for anything.

Biden is an interesting case in that Donald Trump's job approval really fit that low and steady description quite well, where Biden, he actually is losing the enthusiasm and support of some Democrats in a way that Trump never did. The irony of the Trump presidency is that for all that his job approval numbers tended to be pretty low throughout, he also maintained the highest job approval among Republicans of really any president when you look at how their own party viewed them. So, when Donald Trump said he could shoot someone on Fifth Avenue and his voters would stay with him, he wasn't completely wrong in that political assessment. But that does mean that for most presidents, if you've really only got the support of your party, even if that support is quite strong, it keeps your job approval low and steady. So, this has some spillover effect. It reduces the president's mandate. It reduces their ability to strong-arm Congress into doing things because they're very popular. And it reduces their incentives to want to appeal to the other side. If you're the Biden administration, why bother going on Fox, or if you're the Trump administration, why bother sending a spokesperson on to MSNBC. But I'll leave it to other panelists to talk about the aftereffects of what happens when presidents are unpopular.

* * *

Susan Glasser: Kristen reveals a startling new reality via the permanent unpopularity of the American presidency. And it has pretty big implications for just about everything.

Kenneth Baer looks at communications and the modern White House—both from the perspective of someone who was living it as well as how it's changed since then with the Trump presidency—obviously going one way or the other [being] a marker of a very, very different model for presidential communications. But Ken was a founder of the journal *Democracy*, which I always point out because it's a very important publication, especially now that that's no longer an academic interest purely but a day-in and day-out question in our politics, . . . [and Ken] served in the first term of the Obama administration, which is why his paper also includes probably the only history of the OMB [Office of Management and Budget] Twitter feed that you're going to get. I found that to be a really important point about Obama's presidency, coinciding with the iPhone debuting just a few months before the Obama presidency, arguably both those being kind of transformative events in the modern presidency. So . . . how does that connect with this new reality that Kristen is also describing, which is one where polarization means it's very hard for presidents to define leading except in a very fragmented way, the way in which we all experience the media world at this point?

* * *

Kenneth S. Baer, former Clinton and Obama administrations communications aide: We could spend all day arguing which came first, the polarization or the new media, which is affecting whom, but ultimately the polarization is sort of an effect unto itself. But you mentioned the iPhone. Just from my own personal experience, I was a young speech writer for Vice President Gore at the very end of the Clinton years. My first day at work, they handed me a beeper and the beeper from [the] White House Communications Agency would, for people who don't know what that is, vibrate or ping. And it would tell me, "Go to a phone and call this number." And I'd have to go to a payphone. And they used to be in the Metro platforms. I was stuck there, and I'd call them, like, "What's up? What do you need?" And they usually would argue about an adjective or an adverb and some kind of policy document or speech I was writing, but that was it. Fast-forward ten years later, January 2009, and [I] go into the Obama administration. I'm handed a Blackberry, and the Blackberry was now exponentially more interactive. Now, I can get email. So now not only could I be buzzed and say, "Call me," but I could send an email. I immediately react. And so, I spend, for instance, my whole Metro ride to and from the White House, actually, either reading clips and/or responding to inquiries. By the time I'm leaving the White House, towards the end of the Obama first term, everyone's now scrambling for Twitter handles within the White House itself. And to me, that was just sort of emblematic of this march of technology and about how in the twenty-first century communications has changed.

There's so much to unpack there. But I really think to elevate up to the higher level that you're really talking about, obviously there's the rise of digital media, and digital media is already there by 2000. Internet is there; web is there. People are able to read the *New York Times* online. Bill Clinton is the first president to send an email. He was the first one to go online, but it was a very static sort of experience in 2000. It starts ramping up in 2001. And so, you really have two eras, which the Obama presidency sort of straddles. One is what I'm calling a *pre-algorithmic era*, which is basically you have a digital landscape, which is increasing in popularity and is really hallmarked by the barrier to entry to enter the media landscape is now zero. So, people we know, like Josh Marshall of [the website] Talking Points Memo, can decide, "I'm just going to start a website. I'm going to start reporting and putting stuff out there." Opinion journalists like Andrew Sullivan can say, "I'm just going to start blogging." And the blog is here so, ultimately, it's just the same march we've seen, except more and more outlets. And the barrier to create content and disseminate it is now zero. By the time you start going into Obama's second term—and, again, it's not overnight—but by time we get into the second term, it's now the "algorithmic" era of media. And then that is what is shaping our social media platforms. YouTube, Facebook, and Twitter are using algorithms or very sophisticated math computations, which as a communications person that focuses on words. I have no idea how they work, but be that as it may, it works. And they're using tons of data in order to give you what you want and to create information bubbles, and then to also reward things that get more eyeballs—that's the metric. And so how we intersect in that world is becoming more partisan, gets more activity. I like that. I want to hear more of that. Being controversial, being outlandish, being in some ways just demeaning or saying whatever you want could actually get more eyeballs. And that's the thing which is rewarded. In that era, the Twitter era, the relationship to the White House and the media changes. And in that era, which we can unpack more, you really have something where it's extremely easy to get your message out. And especially under the old norms, and then fast-forward to the end of the Obama era, the person that best understands this media landscape more than anyone is Donald Trump, and Trump realizes and knows how to use social media to manipulate basically the media and how to control the news cycle. And that's what he does. If you have no compunction about saying whatever you want, about being inflammatory, calling people names, all that stuff generates heat and generates attention. And this digital media landscape emerges and then changes over time. And now you have this algorithmic era, and it is problematic because [we are in a highly polarized period, and] . . . the people who are online are deeply unrepresentative of the American people. And I'm happy to go into that more, but just briefly: they are just in general younger, wealthier, whiter, much more liberal, and even among Democrats much more liberal. And it creates a strange echo chamber. And I see that reverberates out into our politics and also reverberates into the presidency and arguably could make governance harder as well.

* * *

Susan Glasser: So other than that, everything's just fine. I'm sure we'll come back to this in the course of the conversation, but I was also really struck by the question of what choices are made and how much; therefore, it's just this structural shift in American politics, because there's a structural shift in media and how we communicate versus "what's the choice, what are the incentives?" Barack Obama had Twitter, but he didn't use it the way that Donald Trump chose to use it. Then Trump got turned off. And the question, as we are a year-plus into the Biden presidency, is how much of Trump's use of this communications environment is a new normal, or was it Trump in every way, a departure, so that even if the tools may remain the same, he actually didn't change the template for presidential communications? I don't know the answer to that, but I do think that's a really interesting question for a conversation and a conference dedicated to the presidency. You know, Joe Biden is not a divisive communicator because that's just not . . . his political persona . . . but I don't know. Maybe he's just bad at communicating.

* * *

Kenneth S. Baer: We now know, all of us here know, there are senior members of the White House who are on Twitter and who are engaging even with people and arguing with them to the point where *Politico*, in their wrap-up of the day's news, will tell you, this is what the White House wants you to read . . . because they retweet it, and this is what they don't want you read and what they didn't retweet. And so, it's just becoming such a part of the fabric. But again, arguably, if you are trying to get engagement on a platform like Twitter, for instance, it's hard; you start thinking that's the people, that's the populace. And it is not. It is deeply, deeply not. And one could essentially say that some of the problems the Biden presidency has had is because it's misreading the room, so to speak.

* * *

Susan Glasser: Kristen, did you see anything as you looked at the data from presidential approval ratings that suggests it's not necessarily a straight course ahead toward this sort of polarization and division? Is there a way for someone to overcome it? Biden doesn't seem to; he suggested he would try, but he doesn't seem to have succeeded.

* * *

Kristen Soltis Anderson: I would certainly never want to be in the business of saying that the way things are today is the way that they will be forever and ever, amen . . . . I think because, one, outside events really do matter, you can take a look, for instance, at the job approval that George W. Bush received after September 11th. And that would have been something very hard to predict in the midst of *Bush v. Gore* and the immense division that our country was experiencing around that election and its outcome, its very close outcome. And so external events have the ability to disrupt and drive things in a very different direction. And we don't know what that will look like. I also think that leadership matters and that there's a little bit of this that is "What came first, the chicken or the egg?" Is it that presidents nowadays make less of an effort to win over the other side because it's less possible to win over the other side? Or does it cut the other direction? Is it that because presidents are making less of an effort to win over the other side things just seem more baked-in and polarized than ever? I don't know which direction the causality arrow points on that front. But I would say that the things that are holding presidential job approval in this kind of low and steady pattern right now are pretty big, strong forces. Solving the polarization we are facing is not something I imagine that will happen overnight. But I wouldn't be reluctant to say that I think it's just going to continue on this way forever and ever, because leadership matters and external events matter.

* * *

Susan Glasser: Obama came in and said, "Well, I'm going to overcome these divisions and be a different kind of president." By the end, that was not what he was saying. And so, [given the concerns regarding] where we are right now[,] is it possible to vary from that trajectory?

* * *

Kenneth S. Baer: We should be humble in what we project going forward. However, the great trend of American government since World

War II has been an increase of power into the executive branch that is inexorable. And when there have been times where maybe . . . [its power has moved] back a little bit to the Congress, [specifically] in the post-Watergate era. . . . [But those periods have] been mere ripples [compared to] the larger tide that's going [the other] way. So, I don't think from a governance standpoint that is what has changed. I also think that there's something [else shaping these] trends, and that's actually politics. And again, despite what anyone may think about Donald Trump, and I think extremely low of him personally. However, what is interesting is that what we have seen is that, in both the 2016 and 2020 elections, there are groups of voters whose partisan attachments are in play, who have shifted. . . . There's the white working class. There is the working class broadly of all racial backgrounds, as well as white suburban voters, as we see also some of them in play, which has led to different outcomes in the Congress and, frankly, in the presidency. So, to think that our politics [are] just stuck and static, and it's like a trench between the two. There's actually been some movement, which is interesting. And if that resolves into one large new electoral coalition, I doubt it, but who knows? But if we were sitting here in 2012, who would have predicted ten years later . . . [that] you're going to have, I think it was, 40 percent of Hispanics voting for a Republican—for the Republican—who wants to close the border. That just seems kind of what would have seemed crazy to someone back then.

* * *

Tevi Troy: The presidency is changing. It changes, it seems, a little bit at a time, but when you look over a twenty-year period, it's changed a great deal in ways that have significant implications for all of us, for our lives, and for our polity. We are only scratching the surface here. This is the launch of a program by the Bipartisan Policy Center on the study of presidential leadership. And I'm excited to do it. I will be calling on great experts, such as the ones you've seen today and others in the months ahead. We're also only scratching the surface on this question of the twenty-first century presidency. A lot of us want to have this conversation about what we want out of the presidency, what we can get out of the presidency, and what is the path to get there.

SECTION III

How We Got Here

Expert analysis on the development of the trends in the American presidency over a multidecade period provide an extremely useful perspective. But presidential-level decisions are not made by historians taking a long-term view of the vagaries of presidential power at various points in time. They are made in the moment, under great pressure, and with imperfect information by politicians. Given this reality, it's useful to garner the insights of those who stood by the presidents as they made those momentous decisions. At the time that this first conversation took place, both Press Secretary Jen Psaki and Senior Adviser Cedric Richmond were still in the White House. They have both now left and, given the timing of their departures, must have had their exits in mind at the time of the conversation (despite protestations to the contrary). That said, the fact that they were still on the job at the time of the conversation provides an invaluable window into how senior White House advisers think while there, before gaining the perspective that comes with having one's White House service in the rearview mirror.

The Formers Weigh In

PART 1

The perspectives of former senior administration officials from the five most recent administrations on the emergence of the twenty-first-century presidency.

Jason Grumet, former president, Bipartisan Policy Center: We are creating a new Bipartisan Policy Center Presidential Leadership Initiative, led by Dr. Tevi Troy. A little over twenty years ago, when several of us came together to start what is now the Bipartisan Policy Center, we did it next door in the quirky little Grange Building on the sixth floor, a very narrow building. And it's just gratifying to think . . . twenty years later, now the Bipartisan Policy Center has about 150 proud Republicans and Democrats and Independents who come to work every day to smile at each other and then try to help the country succeed. At the same time, it is humbling to look at the bitterness and the brittleness of our democracy and realize how much work that we still have left to do. But we are a fundamentally optimistic organization that believes in the long arc of American democracy. And we're also a place that rides to the sound of the bugles.

So today we are actually broadening our mission. The goal today is a new initiative where we are going to be bringing together historians and policy experts and strategists and government officials and advocates who are all committed to working to make the presidency resilient and effective and the important respected institution that our democracy requires. It's really remarkable to be able to start this conversation with a group of people who were inside that funny-shaped room where it happens. We are going to hear from folks in the last four presidential administrations who understand how hard this is and who have the opportunity we appreciate to give us a little bit of grounding as we set our sights on helping things work better.

* * *

Steve Portnoy, CBS News correspondent and president, White House Correspondents' Association: I'm just the latest in a very long line of reporters who have stepped up to serve as president of the White House Correspondents' Association. Our organization was founded in 1914 to advocate for the working men, and then they were all men who were assigned by their publications to cover the White House— the history I believe is relevant to today.

President Woodrow Wilson was a haughty former Princeton University professor and New Jersey governor who was deeply suspicious of reporters. The late historian Stephen Ponder wrote that Wilson viewed the Washington correspondents generally as unimpressive intellects concerned with the most superfluous things, with stirring-up foreign conflicts and pushing stories about the president's family members. Wilson found the reporters' questions repetitive, banal, hostile, and the record shows that on November 17, 1913, President Woodrow Wilson, at a press conference, called some of the news fake, a presidential complaint more than a century old. By 1915, so frustrated with the reporters who covered him, President Wilson stopped giving press conferences and later opened up his own government agency to go beyond the filter. The Committee on Public Information, known as the Creel Committee, printed pamphlets, made silent films, and sent speakers all across the country to tout the efforts of the Wilson administration and to build American support for the US engagement in World War I.

As quaint as it all sounds, historians of the twentieth century have written of this nascent outreach effort as a horrible misuse of government power, propaganda aimed at stifling dissent paid for with the unmatched resources that only taxpayers could provide. I can't imagine what those high-minded historians would think of government Twitter accounts today.

Now, I cite all these examples as part of the historical continuum of which we're all a part—in particular, the ongoing efforts on the part of the White House Press Corps [WHCA] to advocate for its historical prerogatives on behalf of the American public. One hundred and eight years after its founding, the WHCA continues to advocate for the working men and women of the White House Press Corps, day by day, event by event, trip by trip. In 2020, we dug deep into our history and leaned on our history as a self-governing body of fierce competitors in a multiemployer environment to institute our own social-distancing rules to get us through the pandemic.

And as you may have heard, we put on a dinner every year. Our annual fundraising event brings in money—enough money to furnish more than two dozen promising young people with scholarships. Presidents since Calvin Coolidge have been attending our dinner to demonstrate their mutual respect for the First Amendment.

* * *

Kelly O'Donnell, White House correspondent, NBC News: I hope maybe someday there will be researchers or historians who will look at what we do tonight and look for some interesting insights about the modern presidency. These two members of the Biden administration will, I think, be able to take us inside the room behind the curtain, tell us about some of the decision-making that happens inside the White House: Cedric Richmond, senior advisor to President Biden, and Jen Psaki, White House press secretary.

Cedric is senior advisor and director of the Office of Public Engagement. And before that, he served the people of Louisiana for more than a decade in Congress. And of course, at that time [he] was also chair of the Congressional Black Caucus. Jen Psaki, of course, has a lot of experience that she brings to one of the toughest jobs in Washington, having been a communicator in the Obama White House in the press shop, the communications shop, spokesperson at the Department of State for John Kerry, and campaigns and lots of background there—a self-described lover of the Olympics.

You are now the White House press secretary, and there are reports that you may be leaving government service and going to work at MSNBC. I'm an NBC News employee. I can assure you, I have no personal knowledge about any of that. Can you tell us anything about that tonight since I have you here? Is there any update, anything you can tell us about your future?

* * *

Jen Psaki, White House press secretary: Not yet. I will tell you that at some point I will not be in this job. Of course, it could be tomorrow if the president fires me after something I say crazy on this panel. I serve at the pleasure of the president. But I haven't set a date for when I will depart. I will say that when I started this job, I made pretty clear I would stay about a year because I have two little kids. They're three and six, which is very small for anyone who has kids. And I knew that I didn't want to miss stuff. And also, it's going to be time for a new voice. So, nothing at this point to announce. But at some point, there'll be another person in this job. [Note: Psaki left the White House shortly after this event.]

* * *

Kelly O'Donnell: Each of you have a role to play sometimes in bringing the president difficult news, difficult information, unpleasant, unhappy information in your roles. We don't get to hear about that much. So, tell us, what is the process in this White House when you have hard news to deliver to the president? Is there a way that you do that? Is there a way that he processes when you have the tough stuff to say?

* * *

Cedric Richmond, White House senior adviser: No, but I find the best thing to do is just be very direct with him and to the point. Don't beat around the bush. Don't try to hide the ball, sugarcoat it, anything like that. Just give it to him straight, and he'll absorb it. I've seen him take bad news in terms of policy. And I've also been in there when he found out colleagues that he used to serve with or have relationships with have passed. And the best thing to do is just be very candid with him and he gives that back to you. So, it's really easy to do it, and he's not intimidating in terms of receiving information, whether it's good or bad. So, it really makes it easy to just get it out in the open and start a conversation. At least, that's how I find it.

* * *

Jen Psaki: Yeah, I found the same thing. When I talked to the president, then the president-elect, and Dr. Biden about this job, what Dr. Biden said to me was, "Please always be direct with us, and please always be straightforward with us. And if there's something bad coming, we want to know." And I took that to heart, and obviously I don't deliver all the bad news—neither does Cedric.

* * *

Cedric Richmond: I don't deliver any bad news. So, I just want you to know that all my news is good news.

* * *

Jen Psaki: That's not true. I will say about Cedric—and this is kind of how these meetings and discussions happen—sometimes you're in a meeting with the president, and I'm sure this happens in other White Houses, we'll learn on the next panel, but where you're talking about news stories or prepping for an interview, and it will go in a different direction, right? About political races or about what-have-you. And he always looks for Cedric because Cedric has been elected before. So, he has a legitimacy that basically none of the rest of us do. He looks to different people for different things, but I've always found you just have to lay it out and be direct with him.

I will tell you, for the reporters in the room, if there's a bad story coming or something that is related to a family member, or somebody [someone] cares about, we'll either call him, or Kate Bedingfield will call him, or we'll just go see him in the Oval Office and tell him about it. So, he knows what's coming.

* * *

Kelly O'Donnell: So, there isn't any collective wincing on the part of senior staff of, oh, this is going to be a difficult day because we have to tell the president this?

* * *

Jen Psaki: Sometimes you take a moment, and you think, "Let's see how this goes." But I think we all recognize that part of our job is to be direct about whether it's good news or bad news or how things are being digested or received. So sometimes it isn't even bad news. Sometimes it's just, well, if you say that, or if you do that, this is how it may be perceived. And that's part of our responsibility too.

* * *

Kelly O'Donnell: When you talk about Cedric having been in the arena as an elected official, I am sure that given your role, you get a lot of phone calls from "Democrat Johnson," "Democrat Smith," from around the country and around the party with lots of good ideas they want to share with the White House. How do you take in that information from members of your party and decide what should be brought to the president's attention? What should just be filtered through White House–staff level? I'm sure there are a lot of people who have good intentions and have their own constituency that they want to bring to the White House. So how do you manage that?

* * *

Cedric Richmond: Well, one, the good news is the president, in his wisdom, did not put me in the legislative shop. So, my official role—I don't have to deal with all my former colleagues, and I'm in political engagement with our allies. But I do receive a bunch of calls from Democrats, but, believe it or not, I receive a bunch of calls from Republicans, too, that I served with, who—I'll get calls from Republicans that I've served with, Democrats that I've served with when they have ideas, sometimes when they have needs. But the one thing I will say, and I can't go back to a whole bunch of administrations like many of you all can. This is my first one. But I've never seen a group that is so complementary to each other. I've never seen a person process information as fast as Ron Klain. You have Jen that handles press. You have [Steve] Ricchetti that manages relationships; Mike Donilon, who's just a strategist. So, we will filter information through us. And if it's legislative, I send it to Louisa Terrell, her way, we'll discuss it. But this team, we kind of know how the president thinks most of the time, so we know how to handle it unless it needs to get to him. So that's how we do it. But many times, we will pass it on to him because he'll process it, give us an answer really quickly, and we don't have to waste so much time going around it. But for the most part, we solicit the input from members of Congress, both Republican and Democrat.

* * *

Kelly O'Donnell: You shared a number of names there that certainly people in this audience recognize. And then for the wider audience, you talked about the Chief of Staff, the legislative affairs director, senior advisors to the president. He has around him friends and confidants who've been with him for years, sometimes decades. You often talk about the fact that the president's been in public life for fifty years. How do you balance having people he trusts and knows with the need to have new ideas, fresh perspective, a willingness to say things to the president that maybe people who've been around him for a long time wouldn't? How do you balance that?

* * *

Jen Psaki: I would say Cedric and I are both relatively new in the Biden orbit. And to me, you look around, and there are people who've been working for him for ten years, twenty years, thirty years—that's a reflection of their commitment to him. I mean, he's not the first president that's had that kind of a dedicated group. But I remember a couple of weeks into the job, and when I was talking to Ron Klain and others about this job, I said, "How will he trust me? He doesn't really know me." I was kind of this person that seemed familiar to him, maybe during the Obama-Biden administration, but how will he trust me and know that I'm going to speak effectively on his behalf and know that he can be candid with me? And I will say that a couple of weeks into the job, I was sitting in the Oval Office, and there's these kind-of two chairs for anyone who's seen pictures of it. And I was sitting in one of these chairs, and we were chatting, and I said, "I hope this isn't a weird thing to say to a president . . ."—now, when you preface it that way, it's a weird thing to say to a president—but I said, "I feel extremely comfortable talking to you." And part of that is because he is somebody who loves people. He is an extrovert, by all definition. It's exhausting to me to even think about how much of an extrovert he is. So, I would say in my experience, he does allow people in as a newbie. I've experienced that. But it is hard in any White House. And I'm sure the next panel can speak to this, to get outside perspectives and to get more voices in there, because there's just the difficulty of surviving the day sometimes.

* * *

Kelly O'Donnell: And because we have you here, and I really want to try to peel back the layer of what it's like to be in those meetings: when you mentioned that, it brings to mind the fact [that] this is a president who has sort-of a touchy-feely nature. He is sort of emotional. He sometimes is colorful, even a little salty in his language at times. Does that exist in meetings? Is there space for people to be a little emotional, a little colorful when you're debating ideas or is it always more formal? Is it always more on the topic only? Or does it have a little freer form?

* * *

Jen Psaki: I would say there's definitely a freer form.

* * *

Cedric Richmond: We have robust discussions.

* * *

Kelly O'Donnell: So, there's some BFD[1] days around the Biden White House.

* * *

Jen Psaki: I don't know what you mean by that. Tell me.

* * *

Kelly O'Donnell: And I ask because I think the creative process and the decision-making process does have a certain connection to how people feel when they're making decisions and when they're able to offer ideas. Is it a constrained environment? Is it free-flowing? That's part of how people process information. So how would you describe how that goes?

* * *

Cedric Richmond: I would say it's definitely free-flowing. And when you have people like Ricchetti, Klain, and Donilon, who have been around him for a very long time, even when it's not senior staff that want to deliver something, they will take it and deliver it to him and give it to him, how they exchange ideas. And he has an openness, even for stuff he doesn't want to hear. He'd rather hear it than not, but we get into lively discussions about policy. And the one thing that you have to be prepared for is for him to get in the weeds about the details of a policy and being prepared to either defend it or push it. But what you see in those moments, he can be tough. He can be direct, but at the end of the day, it's easy to do it because when you know him, you know where it comes from.

And for him, it just comes from a place of concern about other people, trying to make a difference, be transformational. Some people think that's a bad thing. I think it's a good thing, but he really cares about people. So, it's very easy to be in these conversations, even when he's giving you a hard time, that you don't know all the answers that you should, you know where it comes from. It's just easy.

* * *

Jen Psaki: I would say that he goes into the weeds, and sometimes there's information that he wants that may be unknowable in the moment, which is a reflection of him, which is how many bridges in this specific city need to be rebuilt. And even people who were experts on that do not know that in the moment. And you follow up on that.

I will say, in my experience, and I'm in a lot of these policy discussions, too, but what I find he often does is he will kind of quiz me. I have to be kind of ready—have your coffee—on how I'm going to talk about something publicly, because his concern is making sure I'm talking about it in an accessible way. And I remember the first time he did this to me. He's the president; he could do whatever. But we were doing remarks—review prep for remarks—and he said, "Well, how are you going to talk about?" And it was when the American Rescue Plan was being implemented, and we were getting checks out to people. And there was this whole good question at the time: How were we going to get them to people who didn't file taxes? Right. So, he said to me, "How are you explaining this to people?" And I said, "Well, if you're a nonfiler who was"—"Whoa. Nobody knows what a nonfiler is." And I was like, "Okay, okay. Not a nonfiler."

So, point is, I think what we often experience is when he goes to church, which anybody who covers him knows it's typically on Saturday evenings, he usually comes out of the church and talks to some people, either in here or at home. And often whatever they have said to him or asked him, he then says, "Well, so-and-so doesn't really understand what our mask policy is," or, "So-and-so doesn't really understand what this is. And we need to explain that better." So, we experienced that too, the need to be kind of accessible and making our policies come to life for people.

* * *

Kelly O'Donnell: So, the parish caucus is very important?

* * *

Cedric Richmond: He will cut you off mid-sentence and say, "I'm not interested in Washington talk. People need to hear it in plain English." And that is his driving motto, is to make sure that everybody can understand it so that everybody can benefit from what we're doing—at least know what we're doing.

* * *

Kelly O'Donnell: So that's interesting to hear you say that, because I think outside observers would not always view this president as the most effective communicator himself. He has at times been criticized for not being able to carry his message. At times, he's also very folksy and is able to connect with people one-on-one. But this White House has struggled at times with the message on issues, whether it's COVID, whether it's the domestic agenda. You've also been, of course, hit with lots of issues, as every White House is, that are not of your own making, that are the forces that happen to any White House. Do you feel that the president is at times frustrated by how he is perceived as his own messenger?

* * *

Jen Psaki: That's an interesting question. I think every president probably is frustrated at moments when they do not feel like their views, their passions, their policies are being heard and digested. There's lots of reasons for that. There are good questions that, I know this is not a panel about this, but, "Are our long speeches still effective means of communicating with the public?" Probably not. We know that because there's a lot of ways that people digest information. Would he like to be traveling a lot more out in the country? We've been talking about this for a while. Yes.

[In response to your question,] he is. There are limitations that have been imposed upon him and us because of COVID that I think have not allowed people to see at all times what his magic is, right, which is his ability to connect and be empathetic and talk to people and hear their stories. And often a lot of that is just spontaneous, and because he hasn't been traveling much, I think that's been limiting. But I do think the speeches—I mean, we've done fewer speeches in some ways. And like every White House, you're always trying to think about how to break out of the bubble of things. So, I don't know, it's a constant debate.

But as you noted, also, there are realities of what we have to communicate about. And if you're in the White House, you have to communicate about everything happening in the world. You're asked about everything.

* * *

Kelly O'Donnell: And you've been challenged with COVID all the way through with ups and downs on that. And one thing that I've never really been able to ask you about is: Would you consider it a failure of all of the protocols that have been so carefully put in place if the president himself contracts COVID?

* * *

Jen Psaki: No, and we've said this a couple of weeks ago, purposefully because we want the public to understand that he could get COVID. He is double-boosted. We know that being boosted and certainly double-boosted increases your protection from hospitalization and death by many, many decibels. But it is possible he could.[2]

* * *

Kelly O'Donnell: That's a national security event.

* * *

Jen Psaki: Here's what I would say: he's got access to the best health-care and medical care in the world. They have assessed that the risk is worth him going out and traveling this week in the country and doing that. They have assessed, and we know that he can be president wherever he is. That is what the United States prepares any president for.

* * *

Kelly O'Donnell: And do you have a specific plan if he were to get COVID and with all those protections and vaccines, presuming the course of that would not be serious? Do you have a plan for how you would deal with the fact he wouldn't be seen in public for a series of days?

* * *

Jen Psaki: We don't know that that would be the case, right? There's a lot of means to communicate with the public and nothing more to detail here. But what I will tell you is that we want to be clear and transparent with the public that he could test positive for COVID. He does have access to the best health and medical care. There is no secret drug he's taking. He's not immunocompromised. People ask that a lot. I don't know why. And if he tests positive for COVID, we will tell you and everybody about it.

* * *

Kelly O'Donnell: Turning to a different subject. One of the highlights of this presidency so far has been all of the work around the next justice, Ketanji Brown Jackson. And I know that there was a lot of work that happened to prepare for that long before we all knew her name. Could you tell us a little bit about how you look to try to fulfill the promise the president made to have a black female jurist who would be his choice, to find those names, to be prepared, to do the outreach at a time when there was no vacancy? When there were clearly other pressing issues that were dominating the day, but you knew there might be a someday long before we knew what Justice Breyer's plans were. So how did you deal with that?

* * *

Cedric Richmond: I think that goes back to two things, and [my] answer [to] the first part of this is, if the president has a frustration, it's the fact that too many people make the assumption that things just happen. Like we just united the West by accident. No, it was intentional to unite the West, bring NATO together. With Justice Jackson, it was intentional from day one. What people don't talk about is the fact that we've put more African American women on the appellate courts than all other presidents in the history of this country combined. And we did it in a year. And we did it in a year because we were building the bench in case a vacancy came up, we would be prepared. And so that's why, when it came up, we were prepared to vet people. Of course, one was a Judge Jackson, but we knew who was out there. We knew their backgrounds.

* * *

Kelly O'Donnell: Did you feel a sense of urgency at those incremental levels?

* * *

Cedric Richmond: No, we didn't. We just kept our head down and kept pushing more nominees for the appellate court, looking at legal scholars and legal minds around the country, because we knew that the first thing we were going to do was nominate a brilliant woman to the court. She would be a brilliant black woman, and I think that the proof is in the pudding of what he did and the result that we got in the caliber of nominees.

But it was not something that we stumbled upon. It was something that we were preparing for since January 20th at noon. And even before then in the campaign, the president made up his mind that he was going to do this well before he announced it in South Carolina. And Congressman [James] Clyburn told him that he thought it was important for him to make it public, that he had made that decision.

But he recognized early in the campaign that that was a void on the court that needed to be filled. And everything we did was around being prepared for that moment.

* * *

Kelly O'Donnell: You raise a point, that so much of what we certainly talk about is the churn of the day, the very hyper-speed of the news cycle and our collective attention span. But White Houses and senior advisors in White Houses have to work on several threads—the fire that's in front of me today and the things we're planning long term. How do you manage short-term crises, long-term planning when you have some serious headwinds?

* * *

Jen Psaki: I would say what people don't always see goes on in the White House, right? You have the National Security team that's very focused, of course, day in and day out, on Russia and Ukraine. But even in the National Security team, you have people who are not at all involved in Russia and Ukraine and focused on China or focused on a range of issues happening at any moment around the world—Cuban migration talks. And they look at the things that are just in the news in this moment. And what also happens in the White House is there are a range of people who are purely working on domestic issues or working on engaging with the DNC [Democratic National Convention] on what's the future. And so, sometimes what you see and what is understandably dominating the news right now—Russia and Ukraine—it is of course taking up a lot of the president's time. And incidents in the past would have taken up a lot of time of any president, but it's like the tip of the iceberg in some ways of all of the work that is happening every day and every moment.

* * *

Kelly O'Donnell: I could keep going, but I know we have other panels and other presidencies to explore. So, I would like to just ask you each just one last thought. Today, it's fifteen months since you walked in the door, took the oath that you each take as senior advisors. What has stood out most to you that is a surprise about your service and this White House, given all the circumstances that have happened, that you could not have foreseen when you walked in that day? So, one thought that stands out.

* * *

Cedric Richmond: For me, it would just be how intentional it is. And you know, I came from Congress where you just roll with the flow, do what you do. But in the White House, we have a first meeting at eight o'clock. The second meeting is at 8:20. And when we're working on projects, whether it's infrastructure or the rescue plan or others, we meet on that every day. We'll pick a time. Sometimes it's twice a day. With Judge Jackson, we were meeting three or four times a day with inside and outside stakeholders. But none of it is by accident, and it's mapped out. And we meet—as in all of the principals—and what progress have we made? What challenges still exist? And I just didn't know that from the outside. And so, if I ever see President Obama, I probably owe him a big apology because I know how frustrating members of Congress can be now.

* * *

Kelly O'Donnell: There's no recess at the White House.

* * *

Cedric Richmond: There's no recess, but we would call over and be like, we don't understand why this is not done yet. Now I understand that there's a process to it, but just watching how people who have been there before and how we just work, and that's been the most surprising thing to me being in the White House, is just how much focus and intentional actions are done. And then how much you damn meet all the time. But they're meetings with a purpose, like in Zoom meetings. Thank the Lord for Zoom.

* * *

Jen Psaki: I would say I'm incredibly fortunate that this is the second White House I've worked in. And I would say in the first White House, I was just trying to survive. I don't know. I didn't even—I didn't digest things in the same way because I had never been there before. And I remember, not even for anybody who's worked in the West Wing or been in the West Wing, there's a ladies' room on the first floor. I did not know that for the first three years I worked in the Obama White House because you're just trying to kind of survive and be responsive and all the things. I would say I made the intentional decision to be more mindful of taking things in and digesting them and smelling the roses, as my therapist mother would say, as I'm going through this journey. And what has surprised me in some ways is the humanity of all of it. And because you're just surviving, you're trying to be responsive to reporters, you're making decisions on policies—and when you're trying to take in the moments and take a step back, you sit there in the Situation Room where you see the difficulty of things. You see people get emotional when there's troubling, difficult news. You see the president responding in a human way, and everybody doesn't get to see that. And that's one of the things, maybe it's been surprising. I tried to be mindful about taking it in, this journey, the second time around.

* * *

Kelly O'Donnell: Well, thank you for peeling back the curtain a bit.

* * *

Cedric Richmond: So, one thing I'll add, as the new kid on the block, is that there should be an orientation or something. January 20th, at one o'clock, when I got to the White House, they were like, "Your office is 248, 208." But they don't give you a map. The offices don't have office numbers on it. So, I was in there like . . .

* * *

Kelly O'Donnell: It's a sink-or-swim environment.

* * *

Cedric Richmond: [I was] there a week and I was like, "When do we get paid? How much do I make?" They do nothing. And that was my first comment, was, "Look, all of you all have been in the White House before. But not everybody who's here has been here before then." I realized, yeah, I am the only one that hasn't been in the White House before that's in this White House. But there should be some type of mandatory orientation that happens.

* * *

Kelly O'Donnell: I asked Jen about her future. Are you planning to be around for a while?

* * *

Cedric Richmond: I'll be here as long as the president wants me here. I went through the highs and the lows of the campaign. Talk about work, watching him work the rope line at the South Carolina fish fry.

You know, we've had highs, we've had lows, but believing in his desire to be transformational keeps me around every day. And so, as long as he's happy and as long as my seven-year-old, or about-to-be-eight, and saying, "Daddy, it's OK to hop on a plane every week." And part of why the president calls on me sometimes is I'm the only one that flies out every week. And I leave Washington and I go around what other people would call just normal people that are not in the bubble. And so, what I hear out there is far different than what I hear up here. What I hear . . . is the glass is half empty all day long. When I get home, I hear more of the glass is half full and more hope, more optimism. And the best way to know what people are kind of thinking is just to go out there.

So, when I go home, people don't care that I work in the White House. People don't care that I was a former congressman. Certainly, my family doesn't care, but you just get to be around people who are going to give it to you straight. And that, I think, is a value because when you're a senator, when you're a congressman, you go home, and you talk to regular people every day. And that I believe is something that is an asset to the White House, is people's ability to get out of DC and go talk to people who are just busting their butts to make ends meet and keep a roof over their head.

So as long as he wants me here, I'll be here. Now, that could change tomorrow. He could say, "Cedric, you and Jen really embarrassed me." [Note: Richmond left the White House shortly after this conversation.]

PART 2

Previous administration officials share their thoughts: Mack McLarty, Joshua Bolten, Jay Carney, and Kellyanne Conway

Having a senior role in the White House gives people a unique perspective after the intense experience of advising the president of the United States. Departed aides often find that a few major moments stand out. But the length of time that passes after departing the White House has an impact on perspective as well. For those who have left more recently, feelings remain rawer, and regrets loom larger. For those who have had more time since they left, a new perspective emerges, and the impulse to protect the institutions of the presidency appears to take precedence over partisan differences.

* * *

Steve Scully, senior vice president of communications, Bipartisan Policy Center: I am pleased to welcome Josh Bolten, White House Chief of Staff to President George W. Bush. Kellyanne Conway who broke the glass ceiling as the campaign manager for Donald Trump served four years, a front-row seat to the Trump administration. Mack McLarty, who was [a] kindergarten friend of Bill Clinton, White House Chief of Staff to President Bill Clinton. And Jay Carney, former *Time* magazine Washington bureau chief and press secretary to Vice President Joe Biden and President Barack Obama. Thanks for being with us.

Wow. What a panel. The only question I was given in advance is to share with the audience the one story, the one key decision, by the president that you worked for during the time that you were in the White House.

So, Josh, we'll begin with you [and] the decision that George W. Bush made during your time as Chief of Staff.

* * *

Joshua Bolten: OK. And thanks for giving us the question in advance. It didn't require much thought in my case. I served all eight years in the George W. Bush White House. So, I saw a lot of consequential decisions being made, but the ones in which I was most intimately involved were during the three years that I served as Chief of Staff from 2006 to 2009. And during that period, the one that really stuck out for me was a decision that the president made in the midst of the financial crisis to go to Congress and seek what, at the time, was an enormous amount of money. It was over $700 billion to bail out Wall Street and to rescue the country from a much greater calamity than otherwise would have occurred. And it happened at a meeting in the Roosevelt Room. The whole financial crisis is kind of a blur. If you want a good step-by-step history of what happened, then I commend Hank Paulson's book. The [former] treasury secretary wrote a really good book about what happened during the crisis. But for those of us who lived it, it was kind of a blur, which was from my seat as Chief of Staff, Hank would call me up on Tuesday and say that "X investment bank is in some trouble, but we think they'll be OK. And they seem to be working it out." And I said, "Do I need to tell the president, well, just alert him?" On Wednesday, he would call back and say, "It's more serious than we thought, but everything will be fine." On Thursday, he would call and say, "A group of creditors is getting together. We're hoping to organize that, but we're not worried about the solvency of that institution." And on Friday, he would call and say, "I'm heading up to New York to try to rescue a firm."

* * *

Steve Scully: So, the alarm bells were going off?

* * *

Joshua Bolten: Alarm bells were going off all over the place. And there was a cascading, really failure of major financial institutions in the midst of global economic turbulence. It's hard to appreciate today how difficult and dangerous that period actually was. And we were putting Band-Aids on wherever we could. Hank Paulson would run up to New York when he would get with the president of the New York fed, who, at the time, was Tim Geithner, subsequently treasury secretary. And they were trying to save everything.

And finally, Hank concluded that the only way to prevent a collapse of the US financial system was to basically give a bailout to Wall Street. And he asked for a meeting; we convened it in the Roosevelt Room. The president, when he was making decisions during that period, always wanted to have Hank Paulson as treasury secretary, Ben Bernanke as fed chair, and Tim Geithner as president to the New York fed. He wanted them all present. We also had the head of the FDIC and the Securities Exchange Commission. And they were all lined up across from the president. And Hank said, "We need to go ask the Congress for over $700 billion to bail out the banks," which, I mean, no political support for that kind of thing. I mean, all Republicans [were] against it because it was a bailout and all Democrats [were] against it because it was for the banks. The president was well aware of that. And he asked Hank a few questions, and then he turned to Bernanke, and he said, "Ben, what happens if we don't do this?" And Bernanke, who had written his doctoral dissertation on the Great Depression, said, "We are likely headed for a situation similar to the collapse in the Great Depression and possibly worse." And there was silence in the room. And the president said, "Well, I think this makes it kind of easy." And he authorized Paulson to go ahead and go up to the Hill and ask the Congress for $700 billion to be handed out to the banks.

And then when the meeting broke up, the president walked around, and he comforted all of the participants because they were all in shock. It was the last thing you could imagine a Republican administration voluntarily doing. And he encouraged everybody who had had little sleep to go get some sleep. We will get through this. And then when he left the Roosevelt Room and walked across the hall into the Oval Office, I walked back in with him, along with our communications director, Dan Bartlett, and we were quiet for a moment. And he looked at both of us. And he said, "If this is Hoover or Roosevelt, for damn sure I'm going to be Roosevelt."

* * *

Steve Scully: Kellyanne Conway, you've had the unique position of being the campaign manager through the transition and four years in the Trump White House. So, during that time, from your standpoint, the most consequential, the most significant decision that you witnessed or were a part of?

* * *

Kellyanne Conway: It was a privilege to be involved in the Trump White House every day, to work for the country I love so dearly. It's been so great to all of us. I'd say, since you mentioned the campaign and the most consequential decision, there was a selection of Governor Mike Pence as his running mate.

I'd say the most consequential decision that sticks out to me—not consequential, but one that really remains in my head—is international. It'd be taking out of Qassem Soleimani and the entire process that went into that, when the decision was truly made, when the execution happened of the decision and the implications there, honestly, how it was covered versus what it really meant for this country, for the world.

And then I would say domestically, though, the one that really remains in my mind happened in the Cabinet Room on March 2nd, 2020. This is when we had a meeting already set with the heads of the pharmaceutical companies, Gilead Sciences. I believe Pfizer was there. A bunch of them were there, and they came for a drug pricing meeting, which was already a domestic priority of ours that we had been working on for quite a while. Dr. Fauci was there, Dr. Birx. And the president quickly transformed it into a vaccine discussion, and they weren't ready for that. Although in some ways they'd been ready their entire lives for that. And he said, "I don't want to hear that it takes so long. I know how long it usually takes, but you're all telling me, this is the big one that we may be staring down the barrel of a serious, once-in-a-century pandemic. So, if you're telling me that, then I'm telling you, you must develop a vaccine very quickly." And it was explained to the president that therapeutics could be developed much more quickly, something he already knew. And they went through the whole process of that and then, realistically, how much time it would take to develop the vaccine. And some of the more famous doctors said it would take years and years. And he said, "We don't have years," and fast-forward—in less time than it takes to have a baby, trust me, the vaccine was—three vaccines were developed and ready to go into the arms in less time, and did go into the arms and [in] less time, than it takes to have a baby.

But I think that is just a consequential decision, or command, that has saved millions of lives and mitigated a lot of physical damage to many people in this country and likely throughout the world. I think it's a very good example, too, of the volume and velocity with which Donald Trump always wants to operate. It's just this constant flurry of activity. And the worst thing you could ever say to President Trump is that that's never been tried before, or that was tried one time and failed. He believed that his mandate was to get here and keep those promises and do things differently than the way they had been done and then in many ways do things exactly how they had been done. But the therapeutics in vaccines was so key, because he left office on January 20th, 2021, with three vaccines ready to go. And the reason we know that is because twelve million Americans, including President-Elect Biden and Vice President Elect Harris received those vaccines. They were among the twelve million who received them while Donald Trump was still in office. So, I point to that.

The Soleimani take-out was incredibly consequential as well. I know it was covered as trying to be a distraction from impeachment, but it was exactly what you see it being. This president taking out not one, but two, terrorists, al-Baghdadi, of course, and then Soleimani. And then, of course, months later, having Katelyn Mueller's parents be his guests as they had been at the State of the Union, but be his guest at the Republican Convention as well, just to show the real people impact of these decisions.

* * *

Steve Scully: Mack McLarty, when we were talking about this, Tevi was mentioning that it was, of course, Bill Clinton who had the bridge to the twenty-first century, and you were part of that. So, same question, the most significant consequential decision of President Bill Clinton during your time in the White House.

* * *

Mack McLarty: I think it was the economy, stupid, as James Carville famously said. I think our most consequential decision was developing the economic plan, the [Simpson-Bowles] deficit reduction plan, in 1993 and getting it passed. That was the foundation of the Clinton presidency. And I think we saw that in a way that we had not fully expected when we went to our first G-7 meeting in Naples; it was obvious that the world leaders and their finance ministers had taken note—this was a responsible, serious plan that had a possibility to at least slow the growth of the deficit and to help stimulate economic opportunity. And I think that's where the framework to be strong abroad, you have to be strong at home. And to stay strong at home, you have to be engaged abroad. That's really kind of what came out of that meeting.

The backdrop of that, much like Josh was talking about the serious challenge that President Bush faced, was the first Cabinet meeting we convened in Little Rock at the governor's mansion to talk about this economic plan in December. The problem was the deficit was greater than had originally been forecast, which meant President-Elect Clinton would have to seriously consider walking back pledges for a middle-class tax cut in order to achieve the responsible, balanced budget, or at least responsible budget approach. And that was a difficult decision. I will always remember Bob Rubin calling me before that meeting in December with the NASA "Houston" comment: "Mack, we have a problem." That's something you remember. And indeed, we did. The real discussion, as Cedric Richmond talked about so eloquently, was in the Roosevelt Room, which all of us had the privilege of being there. After about six hours of numbing conversations, maybe you don't concern quite the privilege it was when you first walked in the first day. But we went line-by-line on the budget. But before that, we had to have—and Josh, of course, at OMB, you understand it very well, the framework of it—and where we really basically made that decision, I'll always remember it, was right outside the Oval Office. We stepped outside the Roosevelt Room. It was Leon Panetta who was, at that time, director of OMB; Bob Rubin, newly formed National Economic Council,; President Clinton; and me as Chief of Staff. And we were trying to find just that right spot of tax increases, expense reductions—just the right spot for the economic plan. And I think we found it in that hall, and President Clinton kind of went around the group there and said, you know, "Do you agree? Do you agree?" And finally got to me.

And I said, "Yes, I think this is the right place." He said, "Well, I think so too. Let's go get this done."

So, with that, we put the plan forward. We passed it by one vote in the House of Representatives and one vote in the Senate when Vice President Gore voted for us. Now you think about the campaign against President Bush 41, whom I have enormous respect for. Had we not passed that economic plan that early in the presidency, that would have been a significant setback to President Clinton and what we were trying to accomplish. So that, I think, is the most consequential decision, Steve.

The most difficult decision, I think for any president, the most sacred responsibility, is the security and safety of the American people. And that is sending troops in harm's way. Now, we were fortunate. We didn't have to commit troops in that regard, but you did have to commit air cover in a number of instances, both in Bosnia and then the first bombing we did on Iraq after the attempted assassination of President Bush 41. So that's the most difficult decision.

The most consequential, I think, was the economic plan, the deficit reduction plan.

* * *

Steve Scully: Jay Carney, you came to this position in a unique role as *Time* magazine Washington bureau chief. You were a journalist, you served as press secretary to the vice president and then to the president. So again, looking at it through your prism, the most consequential decision during the Obama White House.

* * *

Jay Carney: I was looking down the line here and realizing that I've known each of you for at least twenty years, in some cases thirty, which makes me feel like one of those Washington veterans that they talk about. Again, I want to thank the Bipartisan Policy Center, which hopefully is not an oxymoron. I mean, it's something that we still need to strive for.

A couple of thoughts come to mind, and not really related to my past role in journalism. But many people would say the decision that President Obama made to authorize the mission to eliminate Osama bin Laden was the most consequential decision. It was certainly momentous. After that event, we visited the SEAL team and the commanders who had engaged in it. And one of the leaders came up to me and said, "Your boss has balls of steel." And he said that because he knew that the president had been told that it was basically [a] fifty-fifty proposition that bin Laden was there. And he authorized it anyway with the knowledge that, most importantly, American lives could have been lost—certainly damage to our international relations with Pakistan and other countries would have been harmed. And, you know, the political consequences, obviously of a failed mission and the memory of President Carter's attempt to rescue the hostages in Iran, was not something anybody wasn't thinking about. And yet he made the decision because he believed that the intelligence was solid enough and that the importance of getting bin Laden was so great that we should go forward. And I admired him for that.

I would also say that the decision to go forward with what came to be known as Obamacare, the Affordable Care Act, even when the Democrats lost the Senate. And it seemed like the wise move might've been, the safer move might've been, to do something scaled back. His White House Chief of Staff and others were advising him to do that. And he pressed on anyway, and millions of Americans have health insurance now that they wouldn't have otherwise had, and Obamacare is more popular than ever. And I think that was hugely consequential.

But neither of those are going to be my first choice. My first choice was the decision that he and we together made that has been enormously consequential ever since. And it is, I think in part, one of the factors that has caused some of the increased partisan rancor that we feel today. And that is that we did not take birtherism seriously. We did not believe that people were listening to those folks who are out there claiming that President Obama had not been born in the United States, and that he wasn't Christian, until it was too late. And I know President Obama feels this way because we talked about it. And I know that the polls still show that a majority, a significant majority of self-identified Republicans, don't believe President Obama was born in the United States, and a significant percentage of them believe he was a Muslim. Think about how corrosive that is to our politics, and think about the kind of partisanship that kind of corrosive politics has contributed to what we see today. And that was consequential. That was a mistake. We should have taken it seriously. We shouldn't have joked about it. And you know, perhaps it would have ended differently.

* * *

Steve Scully: You talk about our polarized country and Kellyanne, I guess I turn to you, the fractured media, because any White House is getting a lot of incoming from social media, from partisan media. How do you filter through all of that? How does any White House? And I'd like your response as well. And Josh, mentioned that there was no Twitter really when you were in the White House, but how do you deal with that? Because you were there all four years and you're getting all the incoming, trying to figure out how to sort through it all.

* * *

Kellyanne Conway: Sure. Well, I should probably state for the record that I was offered the press secretary position forty-two minutes after President Trump won election in the wee hours of November 9th, 2016. And I politely declined, and I did many times after that. So, he said, "You'd be great at that." And I whispered to myself, "I'd be a terrible press secretary." I'm not even sure what they do—lots of reasons. I wasn't even sure what they did. I see what they do at the podium, but I'm sure that there's a lot more that goes in. Now I understand what they do—but the point I'm making is, and also communications director. And I also, frankly, think, respectfully to the current administration who brags about it, I think women often get pushed into the scheduling, administrative, and comms and press jobs in White Houses. And I wanted to be a policy person, or I certainly wasn't going to run away from the goldmine of life-changing money I was staring at, and four kids who were crappy ages then and continue to be crappy ages the entire time for a mom to be in the White House. And so, I wanted to work on policy, and I'm very proud and to have a boss who allowed that to be so, but I was also a very public-facing person because the president wants people out there who are able to communicate a message and communicate with people who otherwise may not have that information that day. And that's the key, I think, to the Trump White House, that my audience, people say, "How did you do?" I won't even name them because it elevates them. But, "How did you go toe to toe with that anchor?" or, "How did you really push back on that?" When I say it doesn't even matter who's sitting across me in the anchor's chair or who's on the other side of the blank camera, I can't see. They can see. They're sitting in a studio, they got all kinds of people talking to their ears, looking at teleprompters. People are handing them notes, and I'm looking into a blank camera in the heat, snow, sleet, and whatnot. And they're never my audience. The anchor is never my audience. The audience is the people. And there are people all across this country, ladies and gentlemen, who do not have access to information unless we provide it.

And the one thing I will always credit President Trump for—I write about this in my book—is what I call the democratization of information. So, what happened, because there was no Twitter, we had an awful lot of it. And what happened, though, is whether you like to tweet or didn't like a tweet—and I like to say, "Donald Trump needs to tweet like we need to eat"—it's just about better choices. But when you like the tweet or not, the fact is, is that people received instantly and for free a presidential communication, and it cut out the middleman. So, the middleman didn't like it. But a lot of Americans did because they don't have to pay money to go to a fundraiser. They don't have to know someone who knows someone who knows someone who knows someone to get them the information. It's right there. And if you didn't like it, you can change the channel. But many people felt they learned an awful lot just by having a much more transparent, frankly, and accessible president press-wise.[3]

* * *

Kellyanne Conway: How did I deal with it? I was a lot nicer to people than they were to me and to my family, that's for sure. That'll never change. Some of you in this room, and you know that we see you, and it was completely inappropriate to become so personal to people who were just trying to do their jobs. But how do you deal with it? I think that it's very important, to make sure that there's not information, what I call information underload. I think in our country, we suffer from information underload, and at the White House—or in an administration, a department, or agency—you have a unique opportunity. You have a unique opportunity to cure information underload—of course, [to] cure disinformation as well. And the thirst, I think in our case to sort of—the inclination to want to get the president and not get the story, among some, not most, and certainly all. But it's more fun and actually it's easier. So go for the heat, not the light.

But I think the information underload is a serious chronic problem in our society where we were all inundated with information, but what did we really learn? And so, there's a difference between information education and really trying to sift through that and make it digestible for people who are watching. I mean, did people ever pay more attention or watch every jot and tittle of a presidency? I doubt it, certainly doubt it compared to now. And so, there's that.

And also, managing the press also came with having an excellent and very direct relationship with President Trump, because I'm not speaking up now because I didn't speak up then. God knows I spoke up then. And it is being able to be direct but respectful and deferential to the president of United States, being one of the few people at the beginning of, like, walking in privileges that I would never abuse. People would just walk in or walk through the back doors, just so rude. And nobody ever taught me that. I didn't work in a White House, but I was raised by a woman, not a wolf. So, I just intuited it would be rude to just walk in without an appointment. But having that access to the president, having a president who was not as hierarchical as maybe other presidents, allowed an exchange of information, I think, that was overall beneficial. And I think people having more access to their president, more access to democracy that way is a positive thing.

I'll also say this: that I never, until I wrote this book, never had an agent in my life. I never asked to be a household name and never asked to be well-known. I don't understand the outsize coverage of the "Trump people." It was odd, but he was so different. He was so unconventional, and this country—twice in a row with President Obama, Senator Obama at the time in 2008, and Mr. Trump in 2016, back-to-back—they went for people who were seen as political outsiders who were not seen, who ran on quite successfully in their primaries. And then in the general elections, and twice against Hillary Clinton as being the outsider. And that is an identity that many people in this country share. They feel like they just have their nose pressed against the glass looking in saying, "When is it my turn? What's in there for me?" And then of course we went [an] entirely different direction and voted for somebody who's been in Washington for five decades. So, voters will surprise you, but while we're there, it wasn't even my job, but the president wanted me to do it, and I was happy to do it. And I was happy to do it for the country. Don't be fooled, anybody. I stood out on that—what did they call it? North lawn? I don't know why because there's all gravel, pebble beach sometimes for twenty, twenty-five, thirty minutes at a time, taking lots of press questions and in full view. And I thought it was important to take the questions, even from outlets that weren't particularly kind or fair to my boss or to the rest of us. Because I think it's important to answer those questions. If I didn't have an answer, I said it. I had no notes, no net. And I have to tell you, as a citizen of this country who loves this country and wants any president and vice president to succeed no matter who they are and their party, we can use a lot more of that right now.

* * *

Steve Scully: Josh, I'm going to go back to social media because you really didn't have to deal with that much of it. And Jay, I'd love to get your perspective, because you were fully immersed in it. Has it changed from your perspective, both on the outside and in the inside in terms of how presidents and administrations make decisions, how it may influence the decision-making process? And I would add to that a very fractured media today.

* * *

Joshua Bolten: When you and I talked about this before, Steve, I said I thought that President George W. Bush was actually the last president of the previous century. Because this century of politics really began with the advent of social media, and we didn't have to deal with it. You mentioned Twitter didn't even exist until 2006 and had only a few thousand users. I looked it up. Even Donald Trump didn't have a Twitter account until 2009. So, it was not a factor in the way we went about our business in the Bush White House. But the fracturing of the media already was, so what we're experiencing with everybody having their own channel of communication, which I think has been corrosive for our politics, was already well underway. I agree with Kellyanne that there is a great virtue in being able to communicate directly with the population, that actually we should celebrate that, what technology has brought us.

* * *

But what technology has also brought us is a balkanization of information that has resulted just in the further divisions in our society without even a common set of facts. And that, I think, has been a very bad development for our politics. It is what it is. That toothpaste is not going back into the tube, but we need to find some mechanisms that I know the Bipartisan Policy Center is focused on. So, just the raw antagonism that comes from communicating in 140- or 280-character bites, that attracts attention. We need to figure out how to move our politics away from that, because the trajectory is poor and it's not serving the country well.

* * *

Steve Scully: And Jay, you saw this both as a reporter and inside the White House.

* * *

Jay Carney: When I was at *Time* magazine until the very end, when we started this newfangled thing called a blog. So right before I left to join the incoming Obama administration, it was a weekly in a real way. I mean, weekly deadlines, right. And when I started as press secretary, I remember Robert Gibbs, my predecessor, warned me about this problem, this growing challenge that was social media and especially Twitter, because what it meant, in just a concrete sense, is that when you're doing your briefing to the White House reporters, you spent some time beforehand prepping with various folks from domestic policy, national security policy on the press team, White House counsel's office. And you kind of try to imagine anything that they might ask. And there are some questions that you know were going to be asked because they are the news of the day, the policy of the day, the international crisis of the day. And then you go over others that you suppose could be asked. But you can only know what you know in the moment. What you can't predict, and what I found out very quickly, is when you got up there at the podium and you saw Jake Tapper looking at his phone and then raising his hand and saying, "Jay, it says here that . . . ," and something had happened for which I couldn't have prepared because it hadn't happened before the briefing or that information hadn't gotten out. And so, I think it forced, and I'm sure you've dealt with this Kellyanne, exponentially, just the speed of the information flow was super challenging. And it made it a lot harder to not get tripped up. And it made it harder not to make a mistake.

I remember one of the worst periods I went through as press secretary was the failed launch of healthcare.gov. And it was one of the worst because most of the crises you deal with in a White House, as Jen Psaki was saying, are external. They're things that are happening out there that you're responsible for because you are the White House, and the president's responsible for everything. Rarely do you have a situation like this one where it was wholly our creation. It was the most important piece of domestic legislation that had been passed in decades. And the whole thing was coming apart before our eyes in real time. And I would go up and say—well, because I'd been briefed—"There are some glitches." And I'd be like, "That's not a glitch because Susan Omera in Poughkeepsie can't get on. And she sent me this email and it was a disaster." And that was a case where we couldn't get ahead of the story, because the story was unfolding in real time.

* * *

Steve Scully: President Obama told you privately what?

* * *

Jay Carney: I'll tell you, he's famously even-tempered. But the most angry I ever saw him was in reaction to that, which didn't mean he yelled, because I never heard him yell at anybody. But you didn't want to be on the receiving end for the folks who were responsible for launching healthcare.gov; it was very challenging.

* * *

Steve Scully: So, how did you know? I mean, he didn't scream, but how did you know he was unhappy?

* * *

Jay Carney: In a meeting in the Roosevelt Room, the aforementioned hell chamber that the Roosevelt Room could be, there was a series of meetings about what went wrong and what we were going to do about it. And fortunately, Jeff Zients,[4] whom everybody knows, came in and oversaw a team that, with a lot of tech experts, saved it. But it went on for days and days and weeks before we even knew if it was going to be salvaged. But it's a challenge.

I want to echo something that Josh said, which is there all sorts of problems with social media, but we're not ever going to go back to three networks and a few newspapers. And the wires, Reuters—I see a couple of fabulous Reuters reporters out here and the AP [Associated Press]. That's not happening. And so, we all have to adjust. And I think one of the things that a candidate and then President Trump showed us is that he took advantage of that in a way that I think every politician and every political professional had to take note of, because he was getting right to his audience immediately. And when I started as press secretary in February of 2011, there were two Twitter accounts: @presssec and @whitehouse, right. By the time I left, I think there were maybe thirty or forty among White House staff. But they were still used very carefully. And certainly, President Obama never tweeted without some of us getting eyes on it and vetting it before it went out. And so, there's risk anytime you put too many people up to bat and taking swings and without any controls on it. But you do get injected into the bloodstream very quickly. And we saw how effective that could be.

* * *

Steve Scully: So, Kellyanne, did you ever tell President Trump, "Oh my gosh. Why did you tweet that out?"

* * *

Kellyanne Conway: Yes, of course. Or don't. And you haven't seen those. Of course. Absolutely. Because that's part of the information, that's part of being a counselor to the president—senior counselor to the president. But I did it respectfully and I did it cogently. I'm always surprised, Steve, how people spend what I call their presidential time. Whether you're a senior staffer or, frankly, members of the press, or certainly people who had an appointment with the president for whatever reason, members of Congress, I'm always shocked how they spend their presidential time. Come prepared, have something new and different to say or to offer or to ask. He's already heard all of that. He already saw all of that. It's on all day long in a loop. So, I think this was a president, this is a president who—he's a man who, just once, when he says, "What's going on? What do you hear? What do you see?" And you have an opportunity to say something very different. I would always; I'm a local paper kind of gal. And I would try to read all the local papers across the country to at least see the highlights, to get a digest of those and click onto a few of those. And I was always ready with something like that. Do you remember when you campaigned in Harrisburg? Remember we met the people that they're working on a bill about that? You know, he wasn't like, "Well, who does that effect?" "He was like, "Oh, ok. Should we call anybody? Should we invite them to that thing we're having next week?"

So, on the Twitter question: yes, there were many times. I mean, he once called me down to the office: "The President would like to see you now." And I have my folder, and I'm all ready, and I go down there. I think I have what was Karl Rove's office and Valerie Jarrett's office. It sounds like it's Cedric's office. And it was certainly then First Lady Hillary Clinton's office. Because it wasn't enough, I guess, to be in the East Wing. She had that office, nice office, on the second floor next to the White House Counsel. And I ran down with my folder, and the door was open, and the president was looking at his phone. And he said, "Did you like my tweet?" And I said—I looked around and I said, "Did I like your tweet?" I said, "It takes me twelve seconds to run down here in three-inch heels. Did I miss it?" And chances are I missed it. And he mentioned a tweet from that morning that we had all seen. I said, "Oh, that one. It wasn't in my top one thousand most favorite." And he thought about it, and he said, "Oh, so-and-so called, he really liked it." I said, "Well, so-and-so is an eighty-nine-year-old male billionaire living in Australia. Maybe one day when I'm an eighty-nine-year-old male billionaire living in Australia, I'll like it too." But I took the opportunity to tell him the ones I do like, just the genre of the tweets I think are very helpful in communicating with the public, the facts and figures, or who's visiting the White House. Where are you headed next around the world?—certainly when COVID hit, to make sure that people had that information. Those were very heady times. Those were impossible times. We didn't know what was happening. And we were there twenty-four-seven for quite a while. My seat in the Situation Room was right behind Drs. Fauci and Birx most days. And we were just trying to, as a lay person, trying to figure it out, but then trying to communicate and reflect that to the public.

But there were many. There's an old saying I learned in junior high school English class, that writing is to serve one of two purposes: to get something into the mind of the reader or off the chest of the writer. And that's true of Twitter, as most people in this room know clearly. But I do think Twitter, frankly, as a presidential communication, at least it's part of the record. It's right there. It's probably in the archives now, and he's no longer on Twitter. But I think people using—particularly people using Twitter as a news source is problematic because news on Twitter is different than getting a call and saying, "We're running a story on X, Y, and Z." And we're thinking, "Where did you even see that?" And it turns out it's somebody's comment to a tweet who has fewer followers than I had at my wedding. This is not vetted news. You did not deal with this.

And to go back to your other question, too, Steve—learning what's worth responding to and sifting through, and then just letting other things go because you're just so busy. And I had had lunch with Valerie Jarrett. She invited me to lunch ironically, on January 5th, 2017, before we went in. And I said to her in the navy mess, I said, "What's the most vexing issue to you? What has been most difficult or surprising?" And she said the sheer incoming, how to just keep up with all of that. There are things that you can delegate, but there are so many things that to delegate would be to abdicate—my words, not hers. And she's absolutely right. And I think when you lay on top of that, all the palace intrigue stories and all the "Did you see this tweet?" And there are no editors on Twitter.

And somebody came to my office for a meeting in February of 2017. I was having a really tough first couple of months and lots of people, internal and external—I like to call them enemies—foreign and domestic, wanted me to no longer work in the White House. So, I damn well was sure I was staying for a long time. And this person looked and saw my phone sitting on my desk, and he said, "All those Twitter notifications, they will stop." I said, "I know." I said, "They're so crazy." And he said, "Give me your phone." And he turned off my Twitter notifications. I didn't know you could do such a thing. And even though people had told me "Can you replace Donald Trump's blue bird with a fake one?" many times. And he turned off my Twitter notifications, and they've never been on again in five-plus years. I'm clean. It changed my life. And so, whatever is said about me from people who don't wear pants that snap, button, or zipper, I've never seen. And I feel quite liberated by that. And other people should too.

* * *

Steve Scully: Mack McLarty, Barack Obama famously said, "I have a pen and a phone." One of the things that we have seen is the rise of executive orders by a president trying to bypass Congress. And we know they're short-lived when the president leaves office, but I wonder if you could just talk a little bit about how that has changed the dynamics of the presidency, and is that a troubling sign in terms of the president going above Congress? And I thought the exchange between Kelly O'Donnell and Cedric was fascinating because you really got an insight from both ends of Pennsylvania Avenue.

* * *

Mack McLarty: Steve, on the conversation about all the communication since Al Gore had not invented the Internet when we were in the White House, it's fascinating to me just to watch the thread here of this conversation. Because if you go back to the Bush 41 or prior to that with President Reagan, where the photo op of the day—Mike Deaver's photo op of the day—was how the news was presented. And if you go through that continuum, you'll just see it accelerated. And we thought it was accelerating at light speed in the Clinton administration, as stories would get into the kind of the side press and then the mainstream press. And that continuum, we've just seen . . . an acceleration of the news cycle in different ways to communicate in the weekly versus instantly.

I think this continuum of that is such a central point of perhaps our discussion, a broader discussion. Executive orders, you asked me about. Probably my personal feelings will certainly weigh into this heavily. You know, I was in the state legislature at a very early age with Dale Bumpers as governor of Arkansas. A great, great statesman. I'm just a strong believer in the institutions of our democracy, and I'm a strong believer in bipartisanship. I think I have a record there for many, many years. So, to me, the right way to pass legislation, get support, is to try where possible, where possible, on a bipartisan basis. Welfare reform was a great example of that for us in our administration, as were some other initiatives. The executive order, I think, can be used carefully, sparingly, in certain situations, but where you have, I think, just a really strong number of those legislations or not legislations but decisions and actions. I think it begins to undermine your ability to really galvanize congressional support.

And like all of us who've been in the White House—particularly Josh and I, in the Chief of Staff's office, which was a great, great privilege, rare privilege—you know, I got a Waterford dome from Steny Hoyer that I kept on my desk the full time. Anytime a congressman—like Congressman Richmond, for example—was not in Congress, but someone like him would come in, that showed we understand it's a two-way street between our address and yours. And I think, executive orders, we've got to be very careful and judicious there is the bottom line. That's my personal but strong feelings.

* * *

Steve Scully: Josh Bolten, George Bush said that they took a shellacking in the midterm elections. Kelly was talking about midterm election politics this year. Just kind of go back to how George Bush had to deal with midterm election politics, and yet also deal with the agenda items that he wanted to accomplish. They're not always the same.

* * *

Joshua Bolten: Yeah, they're not. I mean, there is a certain liberation that Mack and Jay had the opportunity to experience being in a second term because the politics are deeply important. They always are, but not having to worry about a reelect is a great liberator for any White House. And so, interestingly, in his first midterm, the Republican Party defied the odds and gained a lot of seats. This was in 2002 in the aftermath of 9/11 when the president's popularity was quite high.

By 2006, the president's popularity was quite low. And I see the Biden people all just crumpled up and the press hounding them because President Biden['s] popularity has fallen below 40 percent. And they're saying, "It's so terrible." And I'm thinking, "What's their secret? How do you get anywhere near 40 percent?" Because by 2006, with the unpopularity of the wars in Afghanistan and Iraq, and in a variety of other things, President Bush's popularity was well down in the thirties, even dipped into the twenties at one point toward near the end of his administration. And that, for somebody like George W. Bush, that had had kind of a liberating aspect. He's a deeply political animal. He cared a lot about the 2006 elections. He didn't go into them with any particular pride of place. If a candidate, as some candidates did, said it's going to hurt me if you show up, he didn't take it badly. He wouldn't show up. For those who wanted and could benefit from his help, he put everything he could into it. But when we took the shellacking in 2006, he didn't go into the fetal position. He'd seen political cycles come and go. And it was always his style to keep eyes forward and try to do the right thing. And that's why I mentioned the second term in particular. There's a certain liberation of just do the damn right thing. Do what you think is right for the country and let the politics sort themselves out. But the politics are about trying to persuade people that you want to do the right thing, that you're acting in their interest. The policy is actually doing what's in the people's interests. And I was super proud to be around the day after Election Day on 2006. Bush was at his desk looking forward, thinking about what's the right thing to do. And then the election after Election Day on 2008, when President Bush, who had supported John McCain—he wanted John McCain to win the election. But he took the remarks that had been prepared for him on the morning after Election Day, and he crossed them out, and he wrote a very, very moving tribute to the American people for the vitality of our democracy and the historic election of our first African American president. And so, politics is one thing. What's good for the country is, I think, in our best leaders, among whom I count George W. Bush. What's best for our country is what counts the most.

* * *

Steve Scully: I have two final points, and I want to give each of you a minute. Can you give us a private moment with Obama, with President Obama, and what would stand out in terms of how he made the decisions or how he filled the office of the presidency—and the same question to each one of you, just a private moment that you could share with us that this audience may not know about President Obama, President Clinton, President Trump, and President Bush?

* * *

Jay Carney: We didn't get an advance.

* * *

Steve Scully: Just popped in my head.

* * *

Jay Carney: A story comes to mind. He [Obama] always sought counsel. He wanted to know what we thought. He often took our advice, but when he didn't, he was very polite about it, but he would tell us that he was going to ignore us, and when Trayvon Martin was killed and, famously, the president went out and said, "He could have been my son." We had met with him in the Oval Office, a handful of us before that, and talked about what he should say, what he shouldn't say, and how personal to make it. And basically, every piece of advice he got was too calculated, too worried, too nervous about the political implications. And he said, "I hear you, but I'm not going to say that." And he gave a little preview of what he was going to say. And then said, "I appreciate everybody in here. Thank you for that. But here's kind of what I'm going to say." And he went out, and I think that was the way he made decisions. He knew ultimately, as everybody that we worked for knew, those decisions were, in the four cases, his alone, ultimately. But they shouldn't be made in a vacuum. They shouldn't be made without expert advice and insight. And so, he sought all of that, but he made clear that there were times that he just disagreed. I mean, we spent, David Plouffe and I, and others, we spent a lot of time giving him great advice about how to win the news cycle that day, how to win the week, how to win the month. And he routinely said, "No, thank you." You know, we thought he was often ignoring great advice, but it just wasn't who he was. You know, like Kellyanne said, he was an outsider. He hadn't been in the game for that long. And he didn't think that way. He thought more long-term, for better or worse politically.

His decision-making process was very deliberate, thoughtful, consultative, and, in the end, very solitary.

* * *

Mack McLarty: I think two moments. One was when President Clinton—and this has been written about—lost his mother. It was a private moment. He called me that night or early in the morning, actually. And I'll always remember.

* * *

Steve Scully: He often did that, right?

* * *

Mack McLarty: And that was not unusual. Donna and I always knew it was Bill Clinton if it was after 11 o'clock at night. That was in Arkansas—after one o'clock for sure in Washington. But his words were, "Mack, we lost her," which we knew was going to happen with Virginia Kelly. The point is, when I got over to the White House to be with him, he really reflected about what his mother had meant to him. I knew that better than most given our friendship, knew Virginia well, a real character, great, great force of personality, tremendous resiliency. But it was a moment for him to take a step back and talk about—I've got to do better, keeping things in perspective. I know that, but I haven't felt it. And I could just see after that moment, his acting and reacting to things just in a slightly different manner. And so, to me, that was kind of the moment I'll remember as inflection point doesn't quite do it justice. It was just a very deeply personal [moment], but a moment that had broader, deeper meaning for his presidency.

The second one, very quickly—I had raised with him that his not being always on time was a serious problem. And I did it with humor. I thought, Kellyanne, that how someone could have such an organized speech that was just beautiful and so organized but could be apparently a touch disorganized, personally, in terms of running on time. And it was in the afternoon in the Oval Office, he had half glasses, and he looked over his glasses, and I could see those eyes there. And I thought, "Well, I've made him mad." And I said, "I see I've made you mad, Mr. President." And he said, "Oh, no, no, no. You just hurt my feelings." The point being: I was not sure since I had never worked for him when he was governor—I had worked with him, I'd been supportive of him, but I had never worked directly in the governor's office—how he was going to take criticism, which I thought it was my responsibility to give him in the right way or a different point of view. And I thought it could, frankly, impair a longtime friendship, which can happen in a White House, as we all know and have seen. Wasn't the case with him. He took criticism well. I think part of it was because he felt like it would not be headlines in the next day's paper. And it was certainly rendered to him in a sincere and respectful manner. So those were the two moments.

* * *

Kellyanne Conway: I have many to choose from, but I think it's important for me to say a little bit about what Mack McLarty just shared with us. I think that great leaders can take criticism, and they almost expect it—not just to accept it but expect it. And one of the most wrong-headed things I believe [was] said about President Trump is that he just wants a bunch of yes men and yes men around him. Actually, obsequiousness bores him because then he didn't learn anything new, he doesn't really know where he stands with you. You're afraid to tell him the truth, or the facts, or the news . . . . We had a lot of churn-and-burn personnel-wise; a lot of turnover. I think many White Houses faced that. This one certainly does as well. But looking back at so many of the people who did not know how to manage the job of being direct and fully briefing the president. So, I think that's important.

It leads me to maybe some of my private moments. I'll pick two; one is quickly. One is just walking into the Oval Office one day and the president was seated there, and they all have big sacks of things to sign. They could be judicial, they could be executive appointments, they could be judicial nominations. That particular day, he had a small folder in front of him, and I can tell he was in a fitted peak. And I said, "What's going on?" And he said, he called me down, and he said, "Do you believe this? How many times am I going to do this?" And I couldn't see from where I was. And I said, "What is [it]?" And I walked around, [and] it was that month's stack of letters to send to fallen soldiers' parents. And he had just had enough of it. He said, "Do you believe we all do this? Every president has to do this. 'Dear Mr. and Mrs. Smith, I'm so sorry.'" He said, "How many times are we to be so sorry?" It really just bothered him. And I think that came from somebody who is the only president, I'm including this one, to not start a new war, but it also came from somebody who, during the campaign, had said, "Listen, folks, if we don't take care of our veterans, who are we as a nation? Here's my ten-point plan, or here's what I'm going to do," which always was a very big policy priority for President Trump. But that just struck me, because it was one of those things where I was walking in early for a different meeting altogether. And he was sitting there just saying, "Can you believe what we're doing?" And I know every president struggles with that part of the job.

The other private moment that I think is such a great-telling American story of how we change our minds, of how we evolve, of how we surprise ourselves with some of our decisions, I think would have to be President Trump's agreement to become the first sitting president in US history to address the March for Life live. And it was shocking to everyone there that President's Bush, in twelve years, President Reagan, pro-life presidents all had never done that. They sort of phoned it in, or vice presidents had never done it. So, Vice President Pence and I had gone [for] the very first time for four or five days, seven days into the administration. But for President Trump to do that in 2018, January 2018, and then to show up in 2020 on the Mall is just remarkable given the fact that for most of his adult life, he had been a Manhattan male billionaire pro-choicer. But it's very telling because he had told me this story in 2011, about how he had become pro-life over time and what his story was. He shared his story of how that happened. Other people have stories regardless of where they stand on that fraught issue. And I loved hearing his story in 2011. He then hired me to do a poll for him. He thought he might want to run in 2012. And I basically said it doesn't look like a very good path. So, he hired a different pollster who told them something different, but here I am. But I think the pro-life story is very important, because him agreeing he could have done what everybody else said, which is "I'm pro-life. I ran on it. I'm going to be with you." But he thought it was important to show up and stand up and speak up on that Mall where thousands of people were that day and had been for many, many years again, through the snow and the sleet and the slights. And I give him credit for that. But it was a big moment. And I believe that the one time with the decision, it was only me there. Another time it was the vice president and two other people in the meeting. And I didn't know we were going to get that agreement that moment that day. You never know what's going to happen.

And I think voters are very smart. They see something in these men—so far, all men—that maybe the rest of us don't sometimes. And they make those decisions thusly. And then, once in a while, something pops up and a decision is made, a statement is issued where you say, "That's why we're here. That's why he was elected."

* * *

Joshua Bolten: Just to add an echo something that both Mack and Kellyanne said, which is that good leaders don't just tolerate criticism, they welcome it. And I think everybody that we worked for did, and we're all better for it.

Private moment, I'm going to mention—well, it's one moment, but it happened many times. And I worked for a president who did commit troops into battle and bore a great burden as a result of it. He did the same thing. He had the same experience as President Trump, but there was a sheet every morning that, during the height of the Iraq War, where the president would get the casualty reports from the overnight, and every morning I saw him circle it. And that's not the moment. The moment I'm going to refer to, the moments that I'll refer to, are the ones that we, in the White House, did not particularly advertise, but the president insisted that whenever he traveled outside of Washington, that the nearest military base be contacted and that he, within a certain radius, that the families of the fallen be invited to come visit with him on his trip. And he did this, I think, well over five hundred times, that he met with families of the fallen. And they weren't to be vetted for whether they were angry at him or supportive of him. They were to be invited to meet with the president.

And, early on in the war, the first time we did this, the proper scheduling way to handle this was we'd arrive at the airfield or whatever, and the president would meet with some people for whatever reason. But now here was this particular reason that he was meeting with a family of the fallen, and then we would go on and do the event. And it was a huge mistake, because the president came out of that fifteen or twenty minutes with the family, weeping with the family. And it was hard for him to do the next event, which might be education or Medicare or something like that.

And so, we rapidly learned that we had to schedule those sessions after he was done for the day—wherever he was traveling to, we scheduled those sessions. And it was the only time, Mack, that President Bush would ever allow us to let him run late, was when he was visiting with the families of the fallen. And more often than not, he would come out of the meetings with the families with tears streaming down his face. It did not shake his conviction that he was doing the right thing for the country. But I mentioned the weeping. I am not a fan of presidential weeping. I don't think we should see our presidents crying on a regular basis. But I mentioned it because I think something that people really need to take account of, that we have all witnessed, is that to be a good president, you have to have empathy for the people you are serving. You have to understand them, and you have to be able to weep with them. And I think those are private moments that were very difficult for all of us, but I think that says a lot about the leaders that we serve and that we deserve in this country.

* * *

Steve Scully: One final question: You don't get do-overs in life. We all make mistakes and try to learn from that. And you probably made mistakes during your time in the White House. So, I want to frame the question in terms of what advice you would give to a future press secretary, senior counselor to the president, White House Chief of Staff, something that you learned on the job that you would then apply to a future White House official.

* * *

Mack McLarty: Well, I think straightforwardly—and professor Martha Kumar and I have talked about this over the years—I think, is to have a well-planned transition. In our case, we did not, because it was a different time and place. It was well before 9/11. Governor Clinton was the underdog early in that race against President Bush 41. And he felt like, as an upcoming governor, if we had a big transition ever, when he was down in the polls, or even when he got up in the polls, worse that some of the press might just write the story. This is a young, overconfident governor measuring the drapes in the White House. Just might've had that story once or twice had that happened. Consequently, after twelve years of Republicans holding the White House with Reagan and Bush 41, we were faced with a very short transition period from November to the swearing-in ceremony to get a full Cabinet government in place and to respond to all of the other demands of that period.

I think since 9/11, you see now a much more formal process. Jason, as you know, you see funding by the Congress for transitions. And I think, Josh, your and Jay's administration are good examples of that. I think the story about the depression with the chairman of the fed is the right story. It was a seamless transition from President Bush 43, from Bush to Obama, with Tim Geithner and Hank Paulson knowing each other. And that's how they should be done. But the national security aspect in the world we're living in makes a transition absolutely essential. So that's the lesson learned.

* * *

Jay Carney: From the perch of being press secretary, I would say, "Take advantage of your predecessors of both parties and seek advice from them." I reached out to all of my living predecessors, and when I left, I offered advice to Sean Spicer and then Sarah Huckabee Sanders. I never heard from them, but I did offer it. But I spoke to most of my predecessors. And you realize that there's so many similarities, that the differences in terms of what policies you pursue or the political positions you take kind of fall away, because the experience is so similar. I also think that it's really important, and I thought it was important when I was there. It's not just the wrong thing to do morally. You shouldn't get up behind the podium or on television and lie, say something you know isn't true to be true.

Now, it doesn't mean that every time I spoke that I never said something that turned out not to be true. But I never said anything that I thought, or I knew, to be false when I said it. And when it turned out I had said something wrong, we would correct it very quickly. It's the wrong thing to do. Our parents told us it was the wrong thing to do, but it really undermines the credibility of the president and the presidency and the administration and the country. So, it's very important. It's better to say, "I'll take the question; I'll get back to you. I don't have an answer" than to guess and get it wrong, and [it's] certainly much better than to just put something out there that's false. Because I think that that is corrosive and damaging to the body politic.

* * *

Joshua Bolten: The advice that I gave, that I have given to some of Mack's and my successors, comes from my own experience as Chief of Staff, and part of the job of a Chief of Staff is to set up the meetings with the president, make sure he's hearing people's views, and that things are well-crafted from the president to make a rational decision. And something I learned early on in my experience is, when people get in the presence of the president, they try to take the edge off the problem, because he's got a lot of things to worry about, and you just don't want to make his life worse. And what then happens is that people have bitter disagreements outside the Oval Office, and they get into the Oval Office. And you know, it's not so bad—well, maybe not in the Trump White House—but they get in there, and they shave the edge off of their advice and they shaved the edges off of their dis-agreements because they don't want the president to have to referee amongst people who have—who have some bitter disagreement and make it make his life harder. That's a huge mistake. And I think when we made mistakes in the Bush administration, it was when we didn't reflect the full depth of disagreement to the president. So, the advice I'd give successors for Mack and me is make it your job when you're in the Oval Office to sharpen the disagreement, provoke people to say what they said outside of the Oval Office to the president, and make his job damn hard, because that is the president's job, is to make the hard decisions. And he should make them knowing what everybody else thinks.

* * *

Steve Scully: Unvarnished.

* * *

Joshua Bolten: Completely unvarnished, if possible.

* * *

Kellyanne Conway: Don't overestimate how much you and your col-leagues and the president himself can get done by this Friday. And don't underestimate how much you can get done in the next one-to-three months. So, I think there's always this rush to solve, to fix, to do, to make better, to check the box off the list. But I think the long view is very important when it comes to policymaking and presidential power. Also, just from my own perspective, but with the gravity and respon-sibility of these jobs must come a certain degree of humility and the more is better, more is better. Don't forget for whom you're working. The oath is not to the president. The oath is not to a political party. The oath is not to the building. The oath is not to your perch in the White House. The oath is to the Constitution. And you're serving the people. And that is very humbling to realize that a decision this way or that way affects so many people's lives or can. And if you don't feel that way and you're offered one of these jobs, or you possess one of these jobs, you really should think about moving on. There are other places and spaces where you belong and will be able to be enveloped and compensated and appreciated, but I think keeping the humility and remembering why you're there, but then also taking the long view, try to do that time and again.

And some of those best laid plans don't happen. I mean, Mack really hit a nerve for me, because if you had asked me what one of the greatest regrets was, I would have said transition because we were all up in New York just a little too long. And this is where transition was. And this is where it was. And this is where our jobs were going to be, but it was just much more efficient to keep the offices going there. And many people from the campaign team were also coming into the White House, etcetera. But I think it's really important to come here to this city and go through those paces. And that is one thing I would say. I would give that advice, saying, "Don't delay that. Don't go and take your family vacation two weeks before you're sworn in, or don't delay coming here from Arkansas or from New York; get here where you're all going to be working together." Because, as Cedric pointed out, I just heard a lot of laughter in the room when he said it. We had said it too. Nobody laughed. At least not with us. There isn't a lot of orientation there. There isn't a ton of on-the-job training when it comes to these positions of great responsibility. You can say "power," but I look at as great responsibility. And so, I did talk to other counselors—people would have that title, people whose portfolio I was about to assume.

And the last advice I would give, especially in these times, and in this town, is it's twofold. Your family and your friends, they're your rock. There are no term limits on them. They really don't care where you work. I mean, mine certainly love it. They're very proud of it, but what do they care? They'll love you most. And they'll be the most honest with you. And get some friends or keep some friends or cultivate some friendships on the other side of the aisle. I have many, and it helped tremendously. It really helped tremendously. It helped them too. And it helped me, but I mean, that is as bipartisan, I would say nonpartisan, as it fundamentally should be, where you have everybody's perspective. And even if people don't agree with you, they will still love you and respect you and appreciate your company and your wisdom. And that's incredibly important for anyone, I think, especially during these times. So, thank you.

* * *

Steve Scully: We are here in part because of Dr. Tevi Troy. He will head up the Presidential Leadership Initiative at the Bipartisan Policy Center. Thank you for a rich and wonderful conversation.

NOTES

1. BFD = "Big f—ing deal," a reference to the comment then Vice President Biden made to President Obama regarding passage of the Affordable Care Act in 2010.

2. Editor's note: President Biden subsequently tested positive for COVID twice and recovered.

3. Transcription text between here and the following question posed to Kellyanne Conway did not register with equipment.

4. Jeff Zients became White House Chief of Staff in early 2023.

CONCLUSION

The Meaning of the Twenty-First-Century Presidency

Tevi Troy

As this volume has shown, the first two decades of the twenty-first century have brought drastic changes to the presidency. Some of it has stemmed from external events. After 9/11, for example, the executive branch under George W. Bush increased its breadth and power in an effort to meet the challenges posed by international terrorism. A new media landscape has meant that the nature of how the president communicates has fundamentally changed. But much of the impetus for change has come from the presidents themselves and their ambitions governing what they wanted to do with the presidency. Barack Obama wanted to find ways to make significant changes to federal policy without being able to pass things through a Republican Congress, so he declared a pen-and-a-phone presidency that sought to do things via executive order that Obama himself had previously declared that he could not do constitutionally. And Donald Trump's "I alone can fix it" mentality signaled his interest in a presidency rooted in unilateral action. And Joe Biden has engaged in an ambitious legislative and administrative agenda that fails to reflect his narrow majorities in Congress as well as, in the case of student-loan forgiveness, existing limitations on executive power.

It is this very combination of a period of great geopolitical and technological change, coupled with presidents who were willing to make significant institutional alterations to the presidency, that has led to

155

this creation of the twenty-first-century presidency. These changes have taken place absent a larger discussion among the American people regarding the appropriate role of the presidency, and this volume therefore wants to begin this conversation by looking at the changes, the factors behind the changes, and the impact of those changes. Therefore, the series of conferences at the heart of this volume were specifically designed to look at these questions from the perspective of presidential experts, executive branch veterans, and in many cases both. Those consulted were from both parties and from various factions within those parties. They served in both pre-twenty-first-century and twenty-first-century presidencies, and this volume shows that they have brought about a fuller sense of what the recent changes to the presidency have wrought.

The volume began with a look at the management of the presidency in this new era, recognizing that presidential decision-making is one of the two key aspects of the presidency. With that in mind, Brookings scholar and former Clinton adviser Elaine Kamarck looked at the increased frequency of implementation failures and the toll they take on public perception of presidential competence. As we ask the presidents to do more and more, the potential avenues for failure expand, with deleterious consequences for the institution of the presidency. Failures eat up a lot of political capital, contributing to electoral failures and hampering presidents in their ability to accomplish their agendas.

One way to protect somewhat against implementation failures is to have a strong transition that can prepare the president and the president's team to handle the enormous challenges of the presidency. As a result, as the presidential scholar Martha Joynt Kumar shows in chapter 2, presidential transitions have necessarily become both more robust and more complex. Over the past sixty years, it has been increasingly seen as the responsibility of the government and not political parties to facilitate the transition from one presidency to another. Yet in our hyperpolarized environment, politics has invaded the previously bipartisan realm of the transition, as Kumar points out, such that only one of the four twenty-first-century transitions in 2009 happened without controversy. While incoming and outgoing teams have put so much more effort, resources, and attention into presidential transitions in the twenty-first century, the paradox is that these transitions have been consistently less smooth and more controversial. Kumar points out that in the increasingly complex twenty-first-century presidency, both incoming and outgoing presidents must be committed to making the transition run smoothly if the new administration is to have a chance at having a team ready to go on Inauguration Day.

The most important thing that a transition will prepare a president for is the national security space. In this area, mistakes are more dangerous and more problematic. As former senior Capitol Hill and White House aide Jonathan Burks shows in chapter 3, the president is typically seen as the sole leader of US foreign policy. However, Burks argues, that is not actually the case, especially in the twenty-first-century presidency when the 9/11 terror attacks served as the catalyst for a change in the relationship between Congress and the presidency on national security and foreign policy. Burks explores several key ways in which Congress exerts its will over the executive branch in foreign policy: through oversight, empowering the executive branch to act more efficiently, war strategy and conduct, international economic policy, controlling sensitive technology, sanctions and other restrictions, and organizational reform. As Burks shows, even in the assertive twenty-first-century presidency, national security is a relationship that is far more complicated than the popular perception that the president is up and Congress is down.

In addition to the management aspect of the presidency, there is also the political aspect. Presidents spend a lot of time and energy on the persuasion part of their jobs. In the twenty-first century, however, there have been massive changes in two key aspects of persuasion: how presidents are measured and how they communicate. With respect to polling, pollster and columnist Kristen Soltis Anderson depicts, in chapter 5, a new normal of presidential approval ratings remaining low and steady throughout twenty-first century presidencies. There are a number of factors involved in this development. There is a general disapproval of institutions across the board. Furthermore, increased polarization has made people more likely to disapprove of any president who does not align with their political identity. While voters often tell pollsters that they value bipartisanship, in practice it is not always rewarded. For this reason, while twentieth-century presidents often had approval ratings over 50 percent, twenty-first century presidents linger—and can even win reelection—with less than majority approval ratings. This development changes how twenty-first century presidents govern, as the importance of maintaining support of a president's own party members outweighs the slim chance of gaining supporters across the aisle.

Kenneth S. Baer, in chapter 6, identifies another change in the way presidents and their teams connect with the people in his paper on communications in the twenty-first-century presidency. Baer, who worked as a communicator in both twentieth-century and twenty-first-century White Houses, describes the shift from a "pre-algorithmic" era in which there is a proliferation of digital media outlets, but social media use is still limited to an "algorithmic" era in which social media platforms predominate. These outlets—Facebook, YouTube, and especially Twitter—are completely different from twentieth-century legacy media outlets, and their influence is so great that they not only shape media coverage but they also shape the actions of the presidency itself. These five aspects of the presidency—implementation, transitions, national security, polling, and communications—provide a useful window into how the presidency has changed in this new century.

These expert views on the presidency provided a quasi-academic perspective on the emergence of the twenty-first-century presidency. Bringing together top officials from recent presidential administrations made the entire exercise more concrete—and more raw. George W. Bush did, as discussed, expand the powers of the presidency, but, as his former chief of staff Josh Bolten explained in chapter 8, he looked at things through the lens of history rather than ideology. When his advisers and staffers warned him that we would head into something worse than the Great Depression if he did not go for a bailout, he went ahead, even if it was contrary to his free-market ideology and perhaps even constitutionally questionable. Obama aide Jay Carney noted that the increased flow of information, thanks to the Internet, has made it much easier for presidents—and their aides—to make a mistake because information gets out quicker than it can be responded to. And Trump adviser Kellyanne Conway talked about the flip side of that issue, which is that the immediacy of social media, especially Twitter, enabled the president to democratize media and make his message more accessible to the public.

Of course, with all of the new developments, some things remain the same. CBS News's Stephen Portnoy observed that back in 1913, Woodrow Wilson called some of the news "fake," showing that presidential dissatisfaction with the media has existed long before the development of our current media landscape. And this very history of the presidency reminds us why these recent developments in the scope of the presidency matter. Our very first president, George Washington, understood that; as he put it, "I walk on untrodden ground."[1] Washington recognized that all of his actions would set precedents and thereby govern the behavior of his successors for centuries to come.

The four presidents of the twenty-first century have all established precedents that their successors will follow. If those successors establish new precedents at anywhere near the rate that our recent presidents have, the mid-century twenty-first-century presidency will be vastly different than the one we have now.

For this reason, the recommendation for future presidents should be to exercise caution in the development of new or expanded presidential powers. By all means, enter the presidency with a bold policy agenda, but do so within the existing parameters of presidential power.

The presidency—and our nation—has existed for these two centuries in large part because the Founders, in their wisdom, established a system in which change would come slowly, with buy-in from both Congress and the executive branch, and with the approval of the judiciary. In recent years, external events, new technologies, and an increasingly impatient populace have allowed ambitious presidents to expand the scope of the presidency. At this point, our presidents and our nation would benefit from a deep breath and an opportunity to understand the scope of the new twenty-first-century presidency without further adding to it.

The presidency is a vital US institution, with symbolic power that can help advance the state of democratic government beyond just the borders of the United States of America. If we lose sight of this fact, and lose control over the scope of the presidency's powers, the implications for both America and the entire world are troubling.

NOTE

1. George Washington, "Letter to Catharine Macaulay Graham," January 9, 1790, Founders Online, accessed August 18, 2023, https://founders.archives .gov/documents/Washington/05-04-02-0363.

About the Contributors

Kristen Soltis Anderson is a renowned pollster, columnist, and radio host. She is a founding partner at Echelon Insights.

Kenneth S. Baer was a senior speechwriter to Vice President Al Gore from 1999 to 2000 and associate director of communications and strategic planning in the White House Office of Management and Budget from 2009 to 2012. He is the founder of Crosscut Strategies and the author of *Reinventing Democrats: The Politics of Liberalism from Reagan to Clinton.*

Jonathan Burks is a former White House aide and chief of staff to former Speaker Paul Ryan.

Elaine Kamarck is a Brookings Institution scholar and a former aide to President Bill Clinton. She was a faculty member at the Harvard Kennedy School of Government and is the author of numerous books on politics and the American presidency.

Martha Joynt Kumar is an emerita professor of political science at Towson University and is the director of the White House Transition Project.

Tevi Troy is a former deputy secretary of health and human services and White House aide and a bestselling presidential historian. He is a senior fellow and director of the Presidential Leadership Initiative at the Bipartisan Policy Center and a senior scholar at Yeshiva University's Straus Center.

Index

163

Printed in the USA
CPSIA information can be obtained
at www.ICGtesting.com
CBHW032325050324
5012CB00009B/106/J

9 780700 636464